THE SMART GUIDE TO

Winning Back Your Time

BY JEFF DAVIDSON

The Smart Guide to Winning Back Your Time

Published by

Smart Guide Publications, Inc.
2517 Deer Chase Drive
Norman, OK 73071
www.smartguidepublications.com

For information, address: Smart Guide Publications, Inc. 2517 Deer Creek Drive, Norman, OK 73071

SMART GUIDE and Design are registered trademarks licensed to Smart Guide Publications, Inc.

International Standard Book Number: 978-1-937636-58-6

Library of Congress Catalog Card Number:

11 12 13 14 15   10 9 8 7 6 5 4 3 2 1

Printed in the United States of America

Cover design: Lorna Llewellyn
Copy Editor: Ruth Strother
Back cover design: Joel Friedlander, Eric Gelb, Deon Seifert
Illustrations: James Balkovek
Production: Scribe
Exective Director: Cathy Barker

TABLE OF CONTENTS

PREFACE

The 21st century, we were foretold, would be characterized by paperless offices, video telephones, and perhaps travel in hovercrafts. As late as the 1970s, some futurists proudly proclaimed that the work week would drop to 35 or even 30 hours and too much leisure time would present a major challenge.

Few people could foresee the impact of the Internet, the "24/7" society, globalization, and other developments that have had a dramatic impact upon us. Society seems to be racing ahead faster than anyone's comfort level, toward ends we can only imagine.

While hundreds of books on time management, software, technological innovations, and other related tools have been created in recent years, when you consider your own career and life, and those of others, it seems there is even more to do than before. Individually and collectively, we are a time-pressed people with apparently no solutions in sight.

You can fantasize about having 36- or 40-hour workweeks, but that's not going to happen. You can surmise what it would be like to be independently wealthy and to not commute to work and fight with all the other salaried drones seeking to carve out a living for themselves. Yet, even if the length of the day was longer and you had multi-millions of dollars, you'd likely discover that the day still seemed to race by.

I maintain that your life will stay the same until you recognize that the sheer number of items competing for your time and attention is increasing at an unrelenting pace. More time in the day, more wealth, or more support services wouldn't be enough for you to stem the tide of the ever-increasing array of news, information, bulletins, broadcasts, competitor products, and service information that finds its way to your mind.

Even if you *knew* that you would live to be 105, having 25 to 40 more years than your counterpart of yesteryear, it would be to no avail if each day raced by at the same speed or faster than it does now.

With this in mind, the only sane route to managing your day, your week, your career, and your life is to recognize that you have to make key choices—choices as to where you will focus your time and attention. You might end up ingesting less information, engaging in fewer activities, owning less gadgets, subscribing to fewer publications, and interacting with fewer people, but that's okay. The quality of your interactions and the quality of your choices is what counts. Less can be more. In a future in which you'll be exposed to more of everything, making critical choices can spell the difference between a hectic, frenzied, time-pressed life and one of relative grace and ease.

Everyone is in the Same Boat

From college students to homemakers to business executives to heads of state, everyone these days needs a little coaching when it comes to staying in control of his or her time. In this book, we'll first take a friendly, in-depth view of the realities that each of us faces nearly every minute of the day. Then we'll move on to solutions to time-crunching situations.

Some of the solutions are ancient, while some are cutting edge. The common denominator is that they work, and they can work for you in the various aspects of your life, whether you are at work, at home, reading, traveling, on vacation, at a conference, or someplace else. I've assembled this book so that you receive top-drawer advice offered with humor and blatant truth.

I've attempted to forsake antiquated clichés about time management and instead offer real-world observations, hands-on suggestions, and practical advice. My mission is to assist you in enhancing the quality of your life for the rest of your life, and to show you that a higher quality of life is obtainable for everyone, based on how you approach each day.

Chapter 1 discusses how leaving the workplace at the "normal" closing time is a fundamental component to getting back in control of your time. Starting with only one day per week and eventually escalating to two or three, by having separate and distinct evenings, divorced from the matters of the workday, you're able to renew yourself in little ways that add up to more energy week in and week out. The chapters that follow tackle a range of common issues such as commuting, being more effective in the workplace, traveling, enjoying, and rediscovering relaxation.

Subtle but Effective

Don't be fooled by the subtlety of many of some of the suggestions. I've learned over the years that the most effective way to help people change is to offer them bite-sized tasks with which they will have a high probability of success. If you try to change too much too quickly, the change doesn't take hold.

Recognizing that your calendar is already full, you are already balancing more than you might care to, and you already have a lot competing for your time and attention, I'll offer tips and recommendations that can become a part of your daily routines.

While not every suggestion is right for every reader, there are enough that will be right for you that this book will be of great utility even after a second and third reading.

As months pass, if you slip a bit in your quest to manage your time, crack open this book to the chapter or page that addresses the issue currently confronting you.

Jeff Davidson

INTRODUCTION

Get in Control of Your Time
(Or Else)

The quest to win back your time is a noble pursuit, but it's a fast-paced and frenzied existence you're enduring. With all that competes for your time and attention, how do you alter the pace of your career and life so you are in control of your time? How can you enjoy what your career and life have to offer, and once again have time to reflect, to ponder, to muse? Keep reading.

You're holding a book about winning back and managing your time. The chances are astronomical that you lost it the last decade. In this book, we'll stay with the tried and true. Some of the tips might seem quite innovative but when I've practiced them myself, and I *know* they work, then it is my duty to offer them to you!

Many people *claim* to being time management or life-balance experts, including authors, speakers, and heck, even talk show guests. Some do quite well in making presentations or in offering the written word.

If I was a member of their audiences or a reader of their works, I would be concerned about what kind of lives they lead. For example:

> What are their tangible accomplishments?
> Are they healthy?
> Are they overweight?
> What are their relationships with their children?
> Are they in a hurry?
> Are they frequently late?
> Do they often lose things?
> Do they work on weekends?
> Do they take trips to expand their horizons?
> Do they take trips abroad?

If they are not able to devote enough time to their families, jobs, health, and continuing educations, then they don't know the art of attaining life balance. They can't talk to you about what it took to "get there" if they are not "there" themselves . . .

Many people who bill themselves as experts in this arena continually juggle every aspect of their lives and "get their act together" only fleetingly. They do so sufficiently enough to convince readers or audiences that they have something vital, yet they lack the nuances or the infinitesimal edge necessary to offer long-term impact.

The Whole Nine Yards

We will examine how to improve the quality of your life for the rest of your life—a tall order to be sure. To achieve all this, first understand that whatever changes you make have to come without too much pain. I know this is contrary to what you've been led to believe about change, but bear with me. If the changes needed to win back your time are too difficult—too many rules, too many things to remember or do—then you're not going to stay with them.

I've observed that simple steps—a moderate shift here, an adjustment there works best in winning back your time. Gradual, subtle, natural changes in what you're already doing yield far greater long-term results. Changes that are radical or anxiety-provoking have much less chance of taking hold. Why? If you've been alive for 25, 35, 45 years or more, it took that long to become who you are and you're clearly perfect at it! You're probably not going to change suddenly in 35 minutes or 35 hours, and, in many cases, not in 35 days.

Whenever you embark upon making changes that are too big a leap from your current ways of doing things, they won't last—or be effective. Therefore, ignore anything that represents too much of a stretch for you right now. Proceed with the suggestions you can undertake most readily. As you initiate more changes, others will fall into place from the momentum of your actions. Gradually, with the proper perspective, a few strategies, and built-in follow-up, you'll win back your time naturally and easily.

This book eases you into each topic as you reclaim your time.

The Gamut of Issues

We'll move from broad-based to nitty-gritty workaday issues; in the last few chapters, we tackle personal perspectives.

Part 1, "The Big Clock is Ticking," takes a look at why you feel mounting time pressure, and gives you definitive strategies for winning back your time. It emphasizes the basic notion of departing from your workplace at a semi-reasonable hour and having the gall to feel good about it! You'll read about pervasive ways that your time becomes used up, why many other working professionals feel almost exactly like you do, and how to assume greater control over your time, more of the time!

Part 2, "Appointing Yourself In Charge," examines how you can determine what's most important to you and what you'll realistically need to do to support your priorities, how much sleep you're getting (which is likely to be way less than your body requires!), the time-money connection, and how to keep others from encroaching on your time.

Part 3, "Taking Back Your Turf," discusses maintaining a reasonably organized office, setting up a home-based office, and managing your files. You'll be exposed to tools to help you be more efficient or (if you don't take advantage of them) fall into an endless well of clutter, confusion, and time-pressure!

Part 4, "Connecting to the World," examines basic problems people face when confronting technology and some options for staying in touch with others without diminishing other aspects of one's life. It also tackles efficiently dealing with correspondence.

Part 5, "Thinking Your Way out of Time Traps," discusses key areas for saving time—making decisions more quickly, honing the ability to focus on one thing at a time, treading more lightly, and constantly reducing what you hold on to.

Part 6, "Your Relationship, Your Time, and Your Peace of Mind," highlights how to carve out time for yourself and for others in your life.

Extras

Throughout the text you'll find boxes with familiar icons and information to embellish what you've been learning, including:

Reflect and Win
New angles on familiar or unfamiliar issues to help trigger the gray matter and prompt you to take action right away, while you're thinking about it.

The Time Master Says
Sage advice and insights from a learned master.

Pause!

A brief idea to keep you on track

Coming to Terms

New words and terms that can aid your overall understanding.

To start right away, flip to Chapter 1 for a look at the reality of how much time you likely have in this life. (If you're lucky, that is!) Otherwise let's roll some credits . . .

ACKNOWLEDGMENTS

Thanks to all the wonderful folks at Smart Guide Publications for having the profound wisdom to publish *The Smart Guide to Winning Back Your Time* and offering key editorial support. Thanks to Cathy Barker, publisher, her insights and guidance, and to Steven Hinkle for timely edits. And thanks to the production team at Scribe..

The Big Clock of Your Life is Ticking

Part 1
The Big Clock of Your Life is Ticking

Your life is finite. It had a distinct beginning and will have a distinct end, unless, of course, if you believe you're coming back as someone or something else. Part 1 offers several hard-hitting chapters that explore mysteries of the ages, such as *why staying at work longer can be self-defeating, quality (versus quantity) of life, how your house got so crowded,* and *slowing down to take a breath.*

CHAPTER 1

The Overtime Epidemic
How to Nip It in the Bud

In This Chapter:

➤ You are doing well
➤ Working too long carries a steep price
➤ Society has become more competitive and demanding
➤ To leave work on time, start with a small step

This chapter leaps right into the issue of overtime, why it can become so troubling, and what you can do about it.

When you examine the big picture of your life and career and your progress thus far, despite the feelings of stress, the frenzy, and the hurriedness, on the whole you've done a decent job of managing your time. Your challenge becomes that of drawing on:

1) your experience,
2) the principles you have developed along the way, and
3) the time management tools and resources at your disposal.

You've got a long way to go in your career and, wherever you're heading, you want to arrive there in style, rested and relaxed, energized and invigorated. Prudent use of your time, all the time, will get you there.

One of the most insidious time traps to which you can fall prey is the belief that by working longer (or taking work home on the weekend) you can finally "catch up." This is a fallacy that will keep you chasing the clock for the rest of your career.

I can sympathize with you if you've found yourself staying at the office later, or toting a bulging briefcase home with you. These maneuvers seem to be logical responses to the pressures you face. For too many people, however, they are also a trap.

Coming to Terms

When something is insidious it causes harm in a manner that is not easily noticed, at least at first. An insidious time trap creeps up on you without you realizing it.

Working Longer is not the Answer

Once you begin taking work home or working a little longer at the office, putting in overtime can become the norm. Soon you're plodding through 30 or 40 pages of reading material, at home each night, as if this habit was necessary.

The Time Master Says

Occasionally it makes sense to take work home from the office. All career achievers do. During specific campaigns (such as the launch of a new business, product, or service), when you change jobs, or when you're approaching a significant event, it makes sense to bone up and spend a few extra hours at work. This needs to be the exception, however, not the rule.

What happens, however, when you consistently work longer hours or take work home from the office? You forget what it's like to have a free weeknight and, eventually, a free weekend! I've observed the working styles of some of the most successful people in Eastern and Western societies: multimillionaires, best-selling authors, high-powered corporate executives, association leaders, top-level government officials, educators, and people from all walks of life. The most successful people in any endeavor maintain a healthy balance between their work and non-work lives.

A Time-Pressured Century

Based on survey information from the U.S. Census Bureau, it's easy to understand why more people in society are feeling more time pressure. The cost of housing rose faster than the rate of wage increase. Commuting time increased more than 10% in the last ten years—not quite a two-minute increase, but spread it across a multi-million person workforce and you see that this increase, within a single, decade represents monumental change.

Telecommuting Doesn't Take Off

What about the potential for telecommuting, i.e. working at home? Most workers are connected to their offices and to the Internet in ways that were simply not available to previous generations. Yet, only a small fraction of the workforce works primarily at home. And, most people have a high social need during the work day . . . few like to work alone.

People are still trudging into work. It is taking them longer to do so; they are exercising less; and they are returning at the end of the day to a home that costs more to live in, is filled with more gadgets, and supports a sedentary lifestyle.

Too Much Competition on All Sides

People aren't working more because they feel like it: our society as a whole has become more competitive and demanding. Employers require more. Kids seem to have to be part of more activities. There are untold types of entertainment options, and the forms of entertainment are proliferating. The video games grow wilder and more complex. "Reality" TV is spreading: *The Bachelor, Mob Wives, The Voice, The Biggest Loser* . . . Text messaging, cyber dating, and all the myriad ways you can be seated at your desk and still have the hours fly by are entertaining, but at what cost? We work more hours, seek to entertain ourselves, try to keep up, quietly go nuts, and consider it normal.

Pause!
U. S. Department of Labor statistics reveal that in the past quarter century, the amount of time Americans have spent at their jobs has risen steadily.

Part-timers, Students, and Homemakers Are Not Exempt

Does anybody get a break in this world? Nearly all the time-pressure problems that plague the denizens of the full-time working world will visit others as well. While you might have extra moments to yourself here and there, everyone who holds any position of responsibility today faces pressures unknown to previous generations.

Reflect and Win

Your quest becomes accomplishing what you seek to accomplish within the eight or nine hours you call the workday.

Your key to reducing the time pressure you feel is not to stay longer at work. Indeed, to reclaim your day you cannot stay longer. This will become clear shortly.

Putting in a Full Day but Not Working a Full Day

Suppose you're among those whose workday is 8:00 a.m. to 5:00 p.m., with an hour for lunch, yielding a total working time of eight hours. Studies show that most people are working only about 60 percent of those eight hours for which they were hired. Even in a tough economy, most people spend three hours and twelve minutes daily not focusing on the tasks, assignments, and activities for which they were hired.

Time Wasted on the Job Mounts Up

Many people don't work a full day, regardless of the number of hours on the job. Suppose someone is on the job eight hours a day. Are they eight dedicated hours? Note: exceptions include the self-employed and the fanatically driven. When everyone around you is fanatically driven, whoa, that can seem normal!

When asked to estimate how much time they waste during a day, most workers are forthright, if widely mistaken, in admitting that it is something above 20 percent. If we use the 20% figure, which is quite conservative, that still means, within a given eight-hour day, one hour and 36 minutes are wasted.

Using the 20% estimate, if 20 people are in your department or division that means you lose 16 hours a day and 76,800 hours in a year consisting of 240 working days. Counting salary, taxes, insurance, and benefits, the typical work hour costs the company $25 to $30; that means that the 76,800 hours lost in a year adds up to nearly $200,000.

So maybe you're not among those who dawdle—and you certainly don't goof off for 20 to 40 percent of your day. Still, it's unlikely that you're working the full eight hours.

Impediments to Working a Full Day

Among the many factors that inhibit your inclination to work a solid eight hours every day are these:

➤ Too many domestic tasks. See Chapter 9, "Buying Yourself Some Time," to learn how easy it is to become stuck thinking that if you spend a few minutes here and a few minutes there taking care of domestic tasks yourself, you can a) stay on top of it all, b) save a little money, and c) cruise into work in high gear.

➤ Not getting enough sleep. Zzzz. See Chapter 10, "Becoming A Snooze-Savvy Sleeper," which discusses why you're probably not getting enough sleep, and how this leads to lack of efficiency and effectiveness.

➤ Over-committing. See Chapter 11, "Loaning Yourself Out Less and Being Happier Because of It," about how widely-available technology gives managers and businesses the opportunity to accomplish more, and also to expect more from their employees— much more.

➤ Not being sufficiently organized. See Chapter 12, "The Efficiently-Organized Office," which explains that a desk is not a filing cabinet, and that window sills and the corners of your room are not permanent storage locations. You can rule an empire from a desk if you know how to do it correctly.

Beyond these factors, over-socializing is the norm in many offices. Some professionals develop elaborate rituals, such as sharpening three pencils, refilling the coffee cup, making a personal call, or waiting until the clock on the wall is at the top of the hour before they start to work. (. . . not something you would ever do, but it happens.)

Eight-hour workdays, of which you have about 250 a year, yield a work year of 2,000 hours. Can you get your job done in 2,000 hours? Yes—2,000 hours, 200 hours, eight hours, even one hour, can be a great deal of time if you have the mindset, the quiet environment, and the tools you need to be productive.

Professor Cary Cooper, an American at Manchester University in England, found that performance declines by 25 percent after a 60-hour workweek. Excess work hours put in by already overtaxed employees are of negative value to an organization when viewed in the context of overall work performance, direct health-care costs, and productivity lost to absenteeism and general lethargy on the job.

Leave Work on Time, Feel Good All Evening

To sustain the habit of leaving work on time, start with a small step. For example, decide that on every Tuesday you will stop working on time and take no extra work home with you. After freeing up Tuesdays for an entire month, perhaps add Thursdays. In another month, add Mondays; in the fourth month, add Wednesdays. I'm assuming there's no way you work late on Friday! (Or do you? If you do, then start with Fridays!)

What transpires in the first month when you've decided that each Tuesday will be a normal eight- or nine-hour workday and nothing more? Automatically you focus more on what you want to complete on Tuesdays. Almost imperceptibly, you parcel out your time during the day more judiciously.

By midday, stop and assess what you've done and what else you'd like to finish. Near the end of the day, assess what more you can (realistically) complete and what's best to leave for tomorrow.

You begin to set a natural, internal alignment in motion. (Sounds exciting, doesn't it?) Your internal cylinders fire in harmony to give you a vibrant, productive workday on Tuesday so you can leave on time.

Pause!
If you deplete yourself of crucial elements to high productivity by coming to work feeling exhausted or mentally unprepared— or if you keep being interrupted— one hour, eight hours, 200 hours, 2,000 hours, or more won't be sufficient for you to do your work. (See Chapter 18 for a simple system to minimize interruptions.)

The Time Master Says
For some reason, once you've solidly made the decision to leave on time on Tuesdays, every cell in your body works in unison to help you accomplish your goal.

A Real-World Approach to Your Time and Life

These resolutions look good on paper, but what about when the boss comes in and hands you a four-inch stack of reports at 3:45 in the afternoon? Or, what about when you receive an
e-mail message, or a memo, that upsets the applecart? These things do happen—and not only to you!

Take a real-world approach to your time, your life, and what you're likely to face during the typical workday. Consider how to approach the predictable impediments to leaving on time on Tuesday.

Rather than treating an unexpected project, dumped in your lap late in the day, as an intrusion, stretch a tad to view it as something else. You got the project because you were trusted, accomplished, or, in some cases, simply there.

CHAPTER 2

Strategies for Survival

In This Chapter:

➤ Stop working at a reasonable hour
➤ Your strategy might depend on your type of organization
➤ Strike a dynamic bargain with yourself
➤ You are not rooted to your desk

This chapter builds on the first chapter, emphasizing the benefits that you'll enjoy once you establish effective procedures for departing from work at a reasonable time.

Now that you know the downside of overwork, as if you weren't already experiencing it, let's focus on the strategies for avoiding it. Begin by taking a small step—stop working *one* evening per week at a reasonable hour. Begin to plot your strategy now: it's your job, and it's your life.

Your Escape Plan and Welcome to It

Here are eight steps to help you:

1. Let it be known that you maintain a home office where you devote untold hours to the organization, after 5:00 each evening. Then, take most evenings off.
2. When you discuss your work, focus on your results (as opposed to the hours you log after 5:00). It is exceedingly difficult for anyone to argue with results.
3. Find role-models—outstanding achievers within your organization who leave at (close to) normal closing time at least a few nights a week—and drop hints about those role-models' working styles in conversation with others in your organization.

4. Acquire whatever high-tech tools you can find that will help you be more productive. If your organization won't foot the bill, do it yourself. Often your long-term output and advancement will more than offset the up-front cost.

5. On those evenings you do work late at the office, be conspicuous. Make the rounds; be seen! After all, if you've got to stay late, at least make sure it's noticed.

6. If zipping out at 5:00 carries a particular stigma in your office, leave earlier. Huh? Yes, schedule an appointment across town for 3:30 p.m. and when it's completed, don't head back to the office. This is a tried-and-true strategy for laggards, but it can work as well for highly productive types like you. If you feel guilty, work for the last 30 or 45 minutes at home.

Pause!

Mr. David Cohn of Surrey, British Columbia wrote to me and suggested an ideal way to ensure that you leave work on time. "If you join or organize a car pool," he says, "you have an irreproachable reason to leave work on time."

Not Everyday is Crunch Time

If you saw the 1985 movie *Broadcast News* with Holly Hunter and William Hurt, recall the scene in which a party is disrupted so the staff can return to the studio to cover late-breaking news. Hunter's character, Jane Craig, takes on the role of a change manager in a crunch time situation.

She starts directing everyone in the newsroom so the station is able to present a timely, professional, and insightful news alert to its viewers. Later, because of her take-charge capability, Craig is promoted to the position of broadcast manager. It's a valuable skill to be able to handle a crunch time situation. Fortunately, unavoidable crunch times tend to come and go, they are always of finite duration.

You don't want to *treat the typical workday like crunch time.*

Pause!

When you do, every day is "crunch time," You start to do foolish things—like throwing more and more of your time at challenges instead of devising less time-consuming ways to handle them—and that means not leaving work on time tonight, tomorrow, or any other night in

Cut a Deal with Yourself to Depart Feeling Good

A masterstroke for winning back your time at any time of day—Tuesdays or any other day—is to continually strike a dynamic bargain with yourself. It's a self-reinforcing tool for achieving a desired outcome that you've identified within a certain time frame, as in the end of the day!

Here's the magic phrase to begin using:

Coming to Terms
A masterstroke is a highly effective or skillful action that one can take.

"What would it take for me to feel good about ending work on time today?"

This is what I mean when I talk about a dynamic bargain. I have this powerful question as a poster on my wall in my office. It can give you the freedom to feel good about leaving the office on time because, when you answer it each morning, you're making that bargain with yourself—you're stating exactly what you'll need to accomplish to feel good about leaving on time that day.

Suppose that today your answer to the question is to finish three particular items on your desk, after which you can feel good about leaving on time. Suddenly the boss drops a bomb on your desk late in the day. You automatically get to strike a new dynamic bargain with yourself, given the prevailing circumstances. Your new bargain might include simply making sufficient headway on the project that's been dropped in your lap, or finishing two of your previous three tasks and x percent of this new project.

Coming to Terms
A dynamic bargain is an agreement you make with yourself to assess what you've accomplished (and what more you want to accomplish) from time to time throughout the day, adjusting to new conditions as they emerge.

TGIF?, You Bet!

The same principle holds true for leaving the office on Friday: feeling good about what you accomplished during the work week. Here is the question to ask yourself (usually sometime around midday on Friday, but even as early as Thursday):

"By the end of work on Friday, what do I want to have accomplished so I can feel good about the week?"

By employing such questions and striking these dynamic bargains with yourself, you can avoid what too many professionals in society still confront: leaving, on most workdays, not feeling good about what they've accomplished, not having a sense of completion, and bringing work home. If you're like most of these people, you want to be more productive. You then want to receive raises and promotions, but you don't want to have a lousy life in the process!

Reflect and Win

Regardless of projects, e-mail, TM, phone calls, or other intrusions into your perfect world, continually strike a dynamic bargain with yourself so you can leave the workplace on time, feeling good about what you have accomplished.

Rather than striking dynamic bargains with themselves, most people frequently do the opposite. They'll have several things they wanted to accomplish that day—and actually manage to accomplish some of them, crossing them off the list. Rather than feeling good about their accomplishments and accepting the reward of the freedom to leave on time, they add several more items to the list—a great way to guarantee that they'll still leave their offices feeling beleaguered. Here you have the ideal prescription for leaving the workplace every day not feeling good about what you've accomplished: if you always have a lengthy, running list of "stuff" you have to do, you don't achieve a sense of getting things done, and you never get any sense of being in control of your time.

Reinforce Yourself for Leaving on Time

When you've made the conscious decision to leave on time on Tuesday and strike the dynamic bargain with yourself, almost magically the small stuff drops off your list of things to do. You focus on bigger, more crucial tasks or responsibilities. On the first Tuesday—and certainly by the second or third—you begin to benefit from a system of self-reinforcement, whereby the rewards you enjoy (such as leaving the office on time and actually having an evening free of work-related thoughts) are so enticing that you structure your workday so as to achieve your rewards.

Coming to Terms

A system of self-reinforcement is a series of rewards you enjoy as a natural outcome of particular behaviors.

Eventually, when you add Thursdays, then Mondays, then Wednesdays to the roster of days that you leave work on time you begin to reclaim your entire work week. A marvelous cycle is initiated. You actually:

➤ leave the workplace with more zest.
➤ have more energy to pursue your non-work life.
➤ sleep better.
➤ arrive at work more rested.
➤ are more productive on the job.

And as you increase the probability of leaving another workday on time, you perpetuate the cycle and its benefits.

Now it's Time to Say Goodbye (for Today)

How do you start this ball rolling? Declare that next Tuesday will be an eight- or nine-hour workday and nothing more. Leave on time that day feeling good about what you've completed. That's it—no grandiose plan, no long-term commitment, no radical change, and 'nary any anxiety.

If you're having trouble giving yourself permission for this one-day, no-overtime treat, recall how long you've been in your profession, and remember that you're in your present position for a lengthy run. On no particular day and at no particular hour are you rooted to your desk. After all, you're a professional. You've gotten the job done before; you'll handle it now as well. Feel free to trust your own judgment about when it's okay for you to go home.

On any given day, when you've decided you're going to leave on time, something could happen to upset your workload so that you have more to do than you can finish that day (and when won't that happen?). The temptation will be to stay late and deal with the new task. Resist it! Instead, map out exactly what you're going to tackle the next morning, in addition to your regular workload. Preparing a plan for tomorrow will reduce any anxiety or guilt you feel about leaving on time today. Ultimately, you'll have little anxiety or guilt. After all, you have a right to a personal life, don't you?

Let everyone in your office know that you're leaving at five, or whatever closing time is for you. Announce to people, "I've got to be outta here at five today," or whatever it takes. People tend to support another's goal when that goal has been announced. Some people could resent you for leaving on time; fortunately, most will not. You have to decide whether to let the resentful attitudes of a few control your actions.

Reflect and Win

Silently repeat to yourself, "I choose to easily leave at closing time today and feel good about it." Never mind if at first, you think this mantra doesn't have any power. Do it. You'll find yourself easily leaving on time more often.

Here's what you can do on that first Tuesday, or any other day, to leave on time when you choose to:

1. Announce to everyone that you have a commitment at 5:30 that evening.
2. Mark on your calendar that you'll be leaving at five.
3. Get a good night's rest the night before, so you'll feel up for the effort of fulfilling your dynamic bargain with yourself.
4. Eat a light lunch; it keeps you from being sluggish in the afternoon.
5. Strike a dynamic bargain with yourself at the start of the day, in late morning, in early afternoon, and in late afternoon. (Remember, it's okay to modify the bargain to accommodate a changing situation.)
6. Regard any intrusion or upset as merely part of the workday, and deal with it. Do not let it change your plans about leaving on time today.
7. After striking the dynamic bargain with yourself, don't be tempted to add more items to your list at the last minute.

8. Envision how you'll feel when you leave right at closing time (but there is no reason for you to be staring at the clock for the last 45 minutes).
9. Need support? Ask a coworker to walk you out the door at closing time.

Ensuring that you leave the workplace on time could seem too involved to accomplish. If you follow only two or three of these steps, however, you'll still attain the reinforcement you need.

The Time Master Says
This chapter is intentionally simple, if for no other reason than this: The more you have to do and remember, the less you'll do and remember. Your only assignment, boiled down to four words is: Leave work on time.

CHAPTER 3

Time Flies Whether You Like It or Not

In This Chapter:

➤ How much longer you're likely to be on this planet
➤ What sucks the time out of your life
➤ Doing what you don't enjoy doing
➤ Simplifying things is vital

In this chapter you'll learn how much time is consumed through various activities in the course of a day, and in the course of a lifetime, and gain a broader perspective as to how to best use the time in your life.

How Much Time Do You Spend on What

Have you ever considered how much time you have in your whole life, and how much time you've spent on various activities? Suppose you graduated from college at the age of 22, and in the course of your life expect to work about 48 years, bringing you to age 70. Over those 48 years, how much time would you suppose you spend on routine activities such as working, sleeping, watching television, recreating, eating, and commuting?

Here's the typical breakdown, based on various demographic studies and my own calculations:

Working	16 years
Sleeping	15 years
Viewing	5 to 7 years (TV, web pages, smart phone screens)
Recreation	2 to 4 years
Eating	3 years
Commuting	2 years

Pause!

The average American will spend 3,000+ hours in the course of a year watching television, listening to the radio, reading, or being online. Since there are only 365 days in the typical year, that means the above activities consume a little more than eight hours per day!

It's amazing when you look at the cumulative total of the time you'll spend engaged in these activities during your productive work life, isn't it? Suppose that you're already 30-something and on average will live another 45 years. Thus, you have about 30 waking years left, and about 20 years to accomplish whatever you're seeking to accomplish. That realization alone might help you focus your time.

If you're thinking, "Hey, I'm 35 now. I don't expect to reach age 80," think again. The Society of Actuaries estimates that if you're female and you're 40 years old, your life expectancy extends well into the 80's, and for males nearly as long.

Data from the National Center for Health Statistics shows that every 25 years since 1900, the life expectancy of both men and women has increased by about five to seven years. The increase in life expectancy for people born between 1975 and the year 2000 was nearly ten years (see Table 3.1).

Table 3.1—Life Expectancy of Americans (from Birth, by 25-Year Intervals)

FEMALE		MALE	
Year Born	Expected Life (in Years)	Year Born	Expected Life (in Years)
1900	48.3	1900	46.3
1925	57.6	1925	55.6
1950	71.1	1950	65.6
1975	76.5	1975	68.7
2000	79.7	2000	74.3
2025	82+	2025	76+

On average, most people are likely to live longer than they think they will. If you think you're going to reach 75, you might well reach 85. If you think you'll reach 85, you might hit 90 or more.

The realization that you might live much longer than you think necessitates developing some longer-term perspectives about how you want to spend your life.

Why Limits are Beneficial to Productivity

Whether life seems short and merry or long and boring, there's only so much of it. Architect Frank Lloyd Wright once observed that people build "most nobly when limitations are at their greatest." You can use the limits on your time or resources to achieve your most desired accomplishments.

Consider how productive you are, for example, before you leave for a vacation, or consider how well you do on a task when a deadline's been imposed (even though you might not enjoy having the deadline or like the person who imposed it). As the author of many books, I can testify about deadlines. Each time I signed a book contract, I had to deliver a specified number of manuscript pages in coherent order and accomplish what I said I would do by a certain date. These contracts with their deadlines imposed limits that actually helped me be productive.

Pause!

Whether you have 30 or 60 years left, it will be to no avail if your days race by, you wake up thinking "I'm already behind," you stay late at work night after night, or you let stuff pile up and then feel exhausted because you can't address it.

These limits might not always appear helpful or supportive, yet you undoubtedly have many of them confronting you. Here are some examples of limits you might be facing right now:

➤ You have to pick your kids up by 5:30 p.m. each weekday.
➤ You have to turn in a work log on Fridays.
➤ The author of this book suggested leaving the office most days by 5 p.m.
➤ You can work about nine hours daily before your mind turns to mush.
➤ Your contract is ending in 11 weeks.
➤ You have only 24 minutes left on your lunch break.
➤ The oil in your car needs changing every 3000 miles or so.
➤ A loved one is nearing the end of his or her life.
➤ You are paid every two weeks.

What limits do you face in your career or personal life that you could employ to propel yourself to higher productivity? When you learn to harness these for the benefit they provide, you begin to reclaim your time. I suggest that your daily, primary limit be finishing your day so that you leave work at the normal closing hour.

Coming to Terms

To harness something is to get it under control.

Time Theft: The Biggest Culprit

After examining the problem for many years, sifting through extensive research, interviewing dozens of people, collecting articles, and tapping the minds of many learned people, I found that the number one element that robs people of their time can be boiled down to a single word. (Be seated in a chair that can support your full weight in case you slump over when the answer is revealed to you.)

Okay, if you're ready, take a deep breath, because here's the revelation of the ages. The number one activity in society, in your life, that steals your time is (here it is—I hope you're ready for this):

Television, and Web-related TV programming

Is it only my perception, or are people now watching TV at all hours . . . *Downton Abbey, NCIS*, NBA games, *Saturday Night Live, Late Night with Seth Myers* . . . And are more people becoming hard of hearing? The plug-in drug has got our culture by the throat. I understand that. The part I don't understand is why the darned things have to be turned up so loud. In addition to becoming intellectually numb, are people also becoming deaf? (Preliminary data suggests that rising noise levels on society *is* resulting in increased hearing loss.)

The Time Master Says

More than 90 million adults watch television at least two hours on any Monday and Tuesday night—that's at least 360 million viewer-hours. These viewer-hours, if applied elsewhere, could transform the nation. Ah, but you can choose to watch TV whenever you want, can't you? Or can you? Television is a drug, with many of the same side effects as other drugs. And as the Internet becomes an even more dominating aspect of more people's lives, it will compete (or merge!) with TV to claim your time.

Endless Entertainment leads to Oblivion

In his book, *Amusing Ourselves to Death* the late Dr. Neil Postman said that entertainment is the dominant force in public discourse in society, affecting the arts, sciences, politics, religion, and education. Certainly entertainment has a necessary function in your life: it stimulates thinking. It can be liberating to your soul. It can give you a break from the monotony of daily living. Entertainment can free you to explore new ways of thinking, new ideas, and new possibilities.

The harm in being over-entertained—which everyone faces—is that your daily life seems to pale by comparison to what you view on the screen. What is the true cost of entertainment? Certainly your time, and usually your money. You're willing to trade these because entertainment expressly is not reality. It's designed to be "superior" to reality—it's more titillating and more engaging. Fantasy sells almost as much stuff on TV as sports, and a lot more stuff than reality ever could. In a 1978 lecture at Indiana University, the late Gene Roddenberry, creator of Star Trek, boldly stated: "TV does not exist to entertain you. TV exists to sell you things."

Reflect and Win

Don't make the erroneous assumption that watching brain-drain TV or listening to shock-talkers on the radio has no impact on your time. They vacuum up time you could have used doing something worthwhile. Turn 'em off.

Our Lives are No Comparison to the Silver Screen

When compared to what you see on the screen, your own life might seem dull and plastic. Instead, it is real and holds great potential. Ultimately, the quality of your life and your memories will depend on what you actively did, not what you passively ingested (such as seeing *Silver Linings Playbook* or *American Hustle* for the third time). What will you do in the next month to enrich your life—actually enrich it? Who will you meet? What will you risk?

Consider how much time and energy you're willing to spend with your favorite TV personalities. Now contrast that figure with how much time you actually spend with any of your neighbors.

You know, those near-strangers next door. Do you even care about their lives? They are, in fact, flesh-and-blood people with real strengths, real weaknesses, and real lives. They could even become your lifelong friends. Do they offer as much pleasure to you, however, as the fantasy heroes you see on the screen?

You might have a reason to like your neighbors: consider all the expensive stuff they're not trying to sell you.

Telekiddies, Hooked from the Earliest Age

Maybe you didn't watch as much television as kids today are watching, but you probably watched a lot, and the habit is ingrained. Kids today, however, are going to set some all-time records. Here's what TV-Free America found about children's television viewing:

➤   The number of minutes per week that parents spend in meaningful conversation with their children is 38.5.

➤   The number of minutes per week that the average child watches TV is 1,680.

➤   50 percent of children ages 6–17 have television sets in their bedrooms.

➤   70 percent of day-care centers use TV sets during a typical day.

➤   73 percent of parents would like to limit their children's TV viewing (but apparently they don't or they can't).

As if you're not watching enough television, what are the chances that you're turning on the radio, cluttering up your mind from that source as well? I know, I know, if you listen to the radio on the way to work, how can that possibly be stealing your time?

Pause!

Dr. James Twitchell, author of *The Carnival Culture*, observed that most American children begin watching television before they can talk, and, by age 6 will have invested more hours watching television they will in speaking with their father over an entire lifetime.
So sad.

Establishing New Routines Yields New Perspectives

Instead of listening to the radio on his drive to work, Bill could contemplate what he'd like to achieve for that day. If he has meetings, he could consider some of the points he would like to make. He might visualize having a pleasant lunch with a coworker. He might put on some classical music to ease his mind as he makes his way through the otherwise-unforgiving rush-hour traffic.

If he consciously chooses to play the radio, maybe he'll switch to a provocative news magazine-type show where issues are covered with some depth and perspective. Perhaps he'll tune into something that truly stimulates his intellect.

Of course, he has the option of playing podcasts or CDs. He can listen to famous speeches, motivational programs, or entire books. By applying a modicum of creativity, he can turn his commuting time into something special.

My friend Bill has many different pockets of time available. He also has many options to determine how he spends them.

So do you.

Jeff Davidson's Ten Steps to Kick Electronic Addiction

"But I'm not giving up television. There are some worthwhile things on TV, and I can turn it off whenever I want." If that's so, then fine. If you're hooked and you can't admit it to me, however, perhaps you can admit it to yourself. Here are 10 techniques you can use to unplug:

➤ Go a whole weekend without turning on a radio or television.

➤ Call your friends (both local and out-of-town) one evening per week instead of watching any television.

➤ Return to hobbies such as stamp collecting, playing a musical instrument, gardening, or playing word games one other weeknight instead of watching TV.

➤ Allow yourself to selectively watch two hours of programming each Saturday and Sunday for one month.

➤ Permit yourself one high-quality video per weekend during another month. The video has to inspire, inform, reflect history, be biographical, or be otherwise socially redeeming. Stop watching shoot-em-ups, chase scenes, and films that titillate but add little to your life.

➤ If you walk or jog, take in what you pass on your trip.

➤ Look for others seeking to wean themselves from electronics. Is there a book discussion group? How about a bowling league, outing club, or biking group?

➤ Attend sporting events rather than viewing the same type of event on television. Watching a good high school baseball team or women's collegiate tennis match can be as rewarding as watching major-league baseball or Wimbledon, respectively. And you visibly support the athletes by being there.

➤ Recognize that the number of DVDs, Mp3s, computer games, and other electronic items competing for your attention exceeds the time you have in life to pay homage to them.

➤ Recognize that rightly or wrongly, you've been programmed since birth to tune in to electronic media for news, information, entertainment, and diversion. It's by no means your only option.

Easy Math for Reclaiming Your Time

While the cumulative impact of being hooked on electronic media is considerable, the cumulative impact of doing what you don't like to do, such as household tasks, is equally insidious.

Recall the example of your 48-year career—graduating college at age 22 and working until age 70. Here's a quick way to see that you need to delegate or cast off those things you don't like to do. Any activity in which you engage for only 30 minutes a day in the course of your 48-year productive work life will take one solid year of your life! Any activity in which you engage for only 60 minutes a day will take two solid years of your 48 years. How can this be so?

Think of it as a mini math lesson: One half-hour is to 24 hours as one hour is to 48 hours. That's true by the good old commutative principle of arithmetic. Likewise, one hour is to 48 hours as one year is to 48 years.

Reflect and Win
Identify those activities you currently handle yourself that could be handled some other way.

For you math buffs, here it is in equation form:

1/2 hour is to 24 hours as 1 hour is to 48 hours, or .5/24 = 1/48

1 hour is to 48 hours as 1 year is to 48 years, or 1/48 = 1/48

When you consume one-forty-eighth of your day (only 30 minutes out of 24 hours) the cumulative effect over 48 years is to consume one year of your 48 years. There's no way around it. If you clean your house, on average, for 30 minutes a day, then in the course of 48 years you've spent the equivalent of one solid year, nonstop, cleaning your house.

If you can't stand cleaning your house (or something else you don't like) for an average of 30 minutes a day, stop doing it. Don't let your house become filthy; hire somebody to clean your house, clean it yourself less often, or find some other alternative. Why? Because the time in your life is being drained; the cumulative impact of doing what you don't like to do, as illustrated above, is that your precious years are being consumed. This is time you simply cannot reclaim under any scenario.

"Well," you say, "that's fine to pay somebody to clean the house, but ultimately I'll be paying people for all kinds of things I don't like to do, so that I can have more time." Yes, exactly. In Chapter 7, "What Matters Most To You?," I'll delve into this in spades.

What things do you know you need to stop doing because they are taking up valuable time in your life? For openers, here are some suggestions:

➤ Cleaning the house.
➤ Reading the newspaper every day. If it makes you late for work or prevents you from handling higher-priority activities, only do it now and then.
➤ Cutting the grass, or any other yard work. (See Chapter 9, "Buying Yourself Some Time," about when it makes sense to pay others to do it.)

➤   Fixing your car.

➤   Cooking.

➤   Reading junk mail because it's addressed to you. (Don't laugh. I know many people who feel compelled to read their junk mail: "Gee, somebody took the time to send me this.")

➤   Reading every godforsaken e-mail message zapped over to you.

➤   Answering the phone.

If you enjoy some of these activities, hey, by all means keep doing them. Perhaps you can do them a little less; perhaps there's another way to proceed. Your goal is to delegate or eliminate those tasks or activities which you can't stand doing. One author advises, "Don't manage something if you can eliminate it altogether." Not bad advice.

What have you been putting off that you could handle right now, knowing you would simplify your life? I won't be offended if you stop reading for a moment, close the book, and give this question the full consideration it merits, unless, of course, a "Family Guy" rerun is coming on.

CHAPTER 4

Time-Binding Dilemmas That Can't Be Ignored

In This Chapter:

➤ Why the time pressure you face is not a personal shortcoming
➤ Other people's time-pressure problems
➤ Five converging factors that conspire to consume your time
➤ More choices than you ever imagined

In this chapter you'll learn how to stay clear of common time traps that lure each of us.

The emergence of the "24/7" society is troubling for many reasons, the least of which is that no one can be up for 24 hours and no one needs to be. So you can order pizza at 3 a.m., shop at the all night store, and surf the web 'til dawn. The key issue is, physiologically can you afford to engage in such activities? Even if you could, why would you want to? Your body needs sleep and regular routines, in a word, predictability. You do have decades to go so don't play beat the clock.

Everyone is Feeling Increasing Time Pressure

Let's consider the two major principles you've been exposed to thus far. From Chapter 1, "The Overtime Epidemic: How to Nip It in the Bud," and Chapter 2 "Strategies For Survival," you learned that the key to winning back your time is to redevelop the habit of completing your work done within the course of a normal eight- or nine-hour workday. In Chapter 3, "Time Flies Whether You Want It To or Not," you saw that even small segments of time each day have a dramatic impact on the amount of time in your life over which you have control.

The dilemma of this entire culture, however, is that everyone is feeling time-pressed—and feeling as if he or she is a poor time manager, as if somehow he or she is at fault. (Do you know the feeling?)

You're not alone. The problem you face is a wide-sweeping phenomenon more than a personal one. Fortunately, there are measures you can take in your career and life to win back more of your time. First, you have to realize the true nature of the situation.

Hurry Sickness Prevails

Suppose that all of society was in a hurry (which at most times seems to be the case)— people having to do more all the time, in less time. Sound familiar?

Some people think that once they retire they will have all the time in the world. Well, you enjoy a little more time, but many retirees say that their days fill up as quickly. You're managing your investments and your garden; you're seeing doctors and your grandchildren; you're keeping up with the news—the day still flies by. The same is true for interns, whether in Washington D.C., corporate offices, or huge medical complexes.

Where Does the Time Go?

Even those not in the work force who volunteer for various causes find that the day is taken up rather quickly. You only have to volunteer for a few groups a couple times a week, and, soon enough, you find yourself roped in. More projects, more causes, more interaction with more people, and, in the end, more to keep up with.

Pause!

For the balance of this book, let's face an ever-present reality: It doesn't matter what your stage or position in life is—old or young, rich or poor, with children or childless—there is more than enough competing for your time and attention.

Time is a Rare and Valuable Commodity

The evidence is mounting that time has become the most valuable commodity in society. People today are craving time to spend with family and friends, and more "free time." They lament having to cut back on sleep to make more time, not being able to make time for great weekends, and constantly feeling under stress.

Pause!

Simply being born into this culture at this time all but guarantees that much of your day will be consumed if you're not careful.

We Want Our Time Back!

Prior to the dominance of the Internet, aspiring professionals faced steep challenges in keeping pace with the developments in their industries. Now, the situation seems overwhelming. You can plan your day with the skill and precision of a surgeon. However, at some point, mail, an email, a text message, a Web site, or a phone call will serve as the tipping point, throwing you off schedule. You have new decisions to make about how to incorporate the new information and handle your time.

Each new intrusion can take anywhere from a few minutes to several hours. Added to everything else you are balancing, even small amounts of information can bring on feelings of frustration and anxiety.

The evil Greek King, Sisyphus, was condemned for all eternity to roll a rock up a huge hill, only to have it roll all the way back down again. Most adults in society also feel as if they are facing a never-ending task. As they draw close to putting their desks and files in order, feeling as if they have mastered the body of information they need to grasp, they are hit by more, and more, and more.

Your email inbox provides the perfect analogy. You can read your incoming mail, and then respond, delete, file, or delegate the messages. However, the task inevitably seems to grow longer and longer each day. The moment when you feel you have everything under control, you log on and become freshly inundated.

Staggering numbers of e-mails are merely a highly visible symptom of a society awash in communication and information overload. The next day, the cycle starts again.

If you're like the typical worker, your day begins with the latest news, weather, and traffic reports blaring from your bedside clock radio. You turn on the TV while dressing, and you scan the latest news appearing on your smart phone while gobbling down breakfast. Then you commute to work. Your work-related messages overwhelm you. You deal with the first message, hoping you can handle some of the others before you have to run off to your first meeting. You temporarily ignore the old messages still awaiting your attention. Your day has only begun, but your constant struggle to manage information is under way.

Who isn't overwhelmed today by information competing for one's time and attention? In my book *Breathing Space: Living and Working at a Comfortable Pace in a Sped-Up Society*, I identify five mega-realities that have an unconditional impact on everybody all the time. The factors include the following:

➤ An expanding volume of knowledge
➤ Mass-media growth and electronic addiction
➤ The paper-trail culture
➤ An overabundance of choices
➤ Population growth

Does it seem as if these factors are ganging up on you? If so, it's time to divide and conquer: Let's examine them one by one.

Too Much Information is Harmful

While information has become easier to find, access, store, and share, concurrently it becomes more difficult to keep up with, manage, and apply in meaningful ways to your career and life.

There is always far more that competes for your attention than you can ever handle. The volume of available information keeps increasing, while the time you have available to absorb it is limited. Few career professionals today have any sense of mastery when it comes to keeping pace with the information they feel they "ought" to keep up with. The flood of yet more information arriving like unrelenting waves wreaks havoc on your ability to engage in quiet contemplation—how to apply what you have learned to the good of all.

An Information Flood Without End

Some people have devised routines to help them make it through the information flood. Many people leave their office in search of a quiet place where they can sit and reflect. Many

Pause!
Here's the impasse of this over-information era: The time necessary to learn all the rules for effective living now exceeds your life expectancy.

carve out times during the day in which they will exclusively open the mail, return phone calls, sift the email glut, and so on.

Just when you put everything in order, the flood of information continues on, and you feel overwhelmed even by midweek. You have chapters of books, magazines, mail, and other stuff piling up that you look at with disdain. So you start again.

Regardless of the ritual, one salient fact remains clear: the amount of information that you're subjected to today is only the tip of the iceberg compared to what's coming. All the management systems, rituals, disciplines, and superhuman efforts to keep up eventually fall to the ever-present reality: there is no keeping up. You need to make tough choices as to what merits your time and attention and have the mental and emotional strength to let go of the vast majority of the information you encounter.

What is Vital to You? What is Not?

Knowledge is power, or so they say, but how many people feel powerful? Do you? Many people fear that they are under-informed. The volume of new knowledge broadcast and published in every field is enormous; it exceeds anyone's ability to keep pace. All told, more words are published or broadcast in an hour than you could comfortably ingest in the rest of your life. By far, America leads the world in the sheer volume of information generated and disseminated.

This is why so many books designed to help readers be more effective in managing their time fall wide off the mark. They list dozens, if not hundreds, of rules. You already have more "rules for being effective" to follow in your career and life, however, than you can comfortably handle. I doubt that feels effective.

The Time Master Says
The key to winning back your time is to be more effective at *being* rather than *doing*. If this sounds like mumbo-jumbo, let me say it another way: Winning back your time ultimately means having less to do, not more. Doing the "less" I'm talking about means carefully identifying what is vital to you, or priorities, which is the subject of Chapter 8.

Understanding the Hierarchy of Input

We have to recognize that less is more, and that we can take in, retain, and use only so much information. Here's a classification system that can help you keep it all in perspective.

➤   Itty Bitty Bits

The lowest level of input is bits, single packets of information that essentially say yes or no, left or right, on or off. In combination, bits add up to data.

➤   Data, Data, Everywhere

Data represents raw numbers in chart form, equations, lists, and so on, and ideally is objective, readily observable, and readily understandable.

➤   Information Abounds

One step up from data is information. This stage represents the manipulation of data, analysis, interpretation, and reporting of data. Most articles that you come across in magazines and newspapers represent information. The author has drawn upon some data or observable phenomena, made some conclusions, and offered commentary.

➤   Knowledge Knocking

When information is added to experience and viewed with reflection, depending upon whose brain is in the driver's seat, it can yield knowledge. Think of knowledge as the culmination of information that somebody gathered, thought about, and started to draw conclusions from.

The most knowledgeable people in your profession, not by coincidence, tend to read considerably, develop original thoughts, and then postulate (and draw conclusions) from what they have taken in.

Comparing knowledge with others makes one valuable both within an organization and with clients and customers. The most knowledgeable salespeople, all other things being equal, have the best chance of achieving greater results. When new knowledge is gathered and added to one's existing knowledge, wisdom becomes possible. This is as true for societies as it is for individuals.

➤   Wisdom Happens

Wisdom often comes slowly, only after years and years of accumulated knowledge. At one time, women could not vote in elections. Ultimately, wisdom prevailed; now it's absurd to think that women would not have the right to vote.

In your career, it's easy to become enmeshed in the over-glut of data and information. It might be temporarily satisfying to maintain an unrelenting pace of reading everything that crosses your desk, downloading files, subscribing to publications, and so on. Indeed, much new knowledge can be generated from such efforts.

Wisdom, in an age in which too much information confronts each of us, often comes in the form of the ability to recognize broad-based patterns and long-term trends, as opposed to being caught up in short-term phenomena and worse, fads.

Drawing Upon Accumulated Knowledge and Wisdom

As you begin to draw upon your own accumulated knowledge and the wisdom that you've develop, you'll be able to free yourself from ever-accelerating flows of information.

If everyone is constantly besieged by information, the most prosperous among us will be those who are able to discern the direction in which society and markets are heading.

As discussed in Chapter 3 (and probably witnessed by you first hand), the negative effect of the mass media on people's lives continues unchecked. The mass media overglut, with its sensationalized trivia, often obscures

Pause!
You cannot read, learn, or absorb information fast enough to keep up. It's humanly impossible.

fundamental issues that do merit concern, such as preserving the environment or feeding the starving. The problem now is that there *always is something on TV that's worthwhile* if not five or six programs! But you've only got one life, can only live it one day at a time, and can only absorb so much.

The number of paper documents within your office is still sizable. The typical executive receives hundreds of pieces of unsolicited mail each month, often more than ten pieces daily. Annually, the average family receives more than 200 catalogs it did not request—add to those the ones it did request, with an onslaught arriving between late August and Christmas.

At home or at work, having too much paper to deal with makes you feel overwhelmed and overworked.

Behind the statistics loom two basic reasons why American society in particular spews so much paper: we have nearly the lowest postal rates in the world, and we have the most equipment that can generate paper!

Choices beyond Counting Is Confounding

Choice is the blessing of a free market economy. Like too much of everything else, however, having too many choices is, well, overwhelming. More than 1,350 varieties of shampoo are on the market. More than 2,000 skin care products are currently selling. Some 100 different types of exercise shoes are now available, each with scores of variations in style, functions, and features. Every choice demands time; increased time expenditure means mounting exhaustion.

Coming to Terms

In *Future Shock* (1970), Alvin Toffler used the term *overchoice* to describe the stress that comes from too many options, especially the so-what variety. In paperback, the book itself was a classic example: you could buy it with a blue, orange, or hot-pink cover.

The Weight of the World is Upon Us

World population grows unabated. In the Philippines, the Manila Hotel provides five-minute helicopter rides for guests between the hotel and the downtown business district. Otherwise, the rush-hour trip would take an hour and a half by car.

Years back, "60 Minutes" reporter Morley Safer narrated a segment on the show that discussed how mass tourism is "turning the world's places of beauty into swarming ant hills and rancid junk heaps." Among the worldwide treasures being laid to waste are these:

➤ Venice is sinking more rapidly than it would be otherwise because of the extreme number of pedestrian tourists.

➤ The Great Wall of China is crumbling under the weight of increasing numbers of tourists.

➤ The face of the Parthenon is slowly but surely being eroded into oblivion.

Reflect and Win

If you feel better about your own life, it's easier to empathize and take action on behalf of those who need help. For one thing, you have a little more time to do so.

Undoubtedly, you've already heard about the number of endangered species throughout the world. This is directly attributable to the increase in human population, increase in development, and clearing of rain forests.

You are less alone more of the time. From the dawn of creation to A.D. 1850, world population grew to one billion. It grew to two billion by 1930, three billion by 1960, four billion by 1979, five billion by 1987, six billion by 1996, seven billion by 2010, with more en route. Geometric human population growth permeates every aspect of the planet: its resources, the environment, and all living things.

The mega-realities aren't likely to diminish but, by understanding them, you're in a better position to take effective action. Read on!

CHAPTER 5

A Crowded House

In This Chapter:

➤ More gridlock in every aspect of life
➤ No clear solutions for decades, so now what?
➤ Increased waiting time is now a part of everyone's life
➤ Patience is a seemingly vanishing virtue

This chapter explores how the effect of rapid increases in population alone has a dramatic impact on the pace of society and your life, and what you can do in the face of this phenomenon.

Predictably, more densely packed urban areas have created a gridlock of the nation's transportation systems. Ultimately, that takes time away from you.

People, Roads, Gridlock and Assault on Your Time

It takes you longer to drive only a few blocks; it's not the day of the week or the season, and it's not going to subside soon. Our population and road use grow faster than the government's ability to repair highways, bridges, and vital urban arteries.

The roads aren't going to clear up soon; it would cost far more than $2 trillion over the next 30 years to repair and maintain the nation's pipes, tunnels, cables, and roads. More than half of the heavily traveled roads in America that link urban and suburban areas are in fair to poor condition. Is it any wonder you lose a good chunk of your time commuting to work and back?

Coming to Terms

The mere word "gridlock," signals that it pays to be a contrarian . . . means someone too obstinate to do what everyone else is seeking to do at the same time.

Commuting snarls are increasing. City planners report no clear solution to gridlock for decades, and population studies reveal that the nation's metropolitan areas will become home to an even greater percentage of the population.

Crowding makes urban spaces harder to traverse, which eats up more time; hence, the less space, the more time consumed. Even suburban areas will face unending traffic dilemmas. If only the gridlock were confined to commuter arteries. Not so. Air travelers, vacationers, even campers—everyone in motion—is (or will be) feeling its effects. Consider some of these "locks" on your time.

➤   Airlock

If you haven't noticed, airline passenger traffic is arduous. Concurrently, there are fewer nonstop flights, particularly on cross-continental trips. Airport expansion trails the increased passenger loads. Worse, all airlines pad their scheduled departure and arrival times—extended more than 50 percent in recent decades—to appear as if they're not late, while actual air time remains about the same. When you're scheduled to board at 10:10 a.m., that is simply when you're supposed to be seated in the plane. Rollout from the gate is always later. Consequently they're as slow and late as ever, but now they're within the promised limits.

➤   Camplock

On an average summer day, Yellowstone Park has more visitors than the population of Houston. Other national parks across the country are faced with swarms of visitors; campsites are in high demand. Vacationers have to contend with traffic, lines for concessions, and waiting lists for campsites.

Hereafter it might make sense to do your camping Tuesday through Thursday—whenever the masses are not there—or find "undiscovered" parks closer to home.

➤   Shoplock

Despite the dramatic increase in online, catalog, and home shopping networks, shopping malls still always appear crowded. Hunting for a parking space can take several minutes, unless you're willing to park in the far reaches of some lots. Once inside, you have to jostle through crowds to reach to shops, movie theaters, and restaurants—and that's on slow days. You experience the worst during the holidays.

Reflect and Win
To avoid the locks that so many others encounter, commute, fly, camp, and dine at different times.

Having to Wait Is on the Increase

Any way you slice it, waiting is going to be a part of your life. Some varieties of waiting are not so bad. Waiting at either your home or office for someone to arrive affords you the opportunity to take care of other tasks, although you still might feel imposed upon.

Delays Away From Your Turf

Experiencing a delay away from your own turf potentially has a different impact. Let's examine three delays frequently occurring outside of your immediate environment and how they are commonly perceived:

➤   Waiting to see a service professional—Delays incurred by waiting to see a doctor or a lawyer, as long as the length of the wait remains within acceptable limits, usually don't throw people off stride.

➤   Waiting for an appointment—Beyond a reasonable threshold, waiting for a service provider or anyone else to come to you begins to feel like an imposition, and each passing minute can seem like two or three times what it actually is.

➤   Unforeseen delays—These can easily be the most frustrating kinds of delays. For instance, you expected to simply dash in and out of the convenience store; however, you experience a seven-minute delay. Those seven minutes seem infinitely longer than other seven-minute segments in your life. And a series of unrelated delays can make each successive delay more untenable!

Delay-Lengthening Culprits

A delay will seem longer when you feel it's unjustified. Take the case of a hotel clerk answering the phone before tending to you. Why would somebody calling be more important than someone who is standing at the hotel registration desk?

A wait under less than favorable circumstances such as humid weather, amidst disruptive noise, or in an inhospitable setting will seem longer. When you are anxious or under stress, any delay could seem long.

What? Me Have Down Time?

Personal technologies have greatly affected people's inability to wait. When you can change channels or Web sites with a single click, why would you want to spend an extra minute in a supermarket checkout line? Patience is seemingly a virtue.

Much of the fascination and over-use of smart phones stems from users' inability to incur any down time, let alone delays or waiting time. Yet, by reflexively stuffing all spare moments with filler phone calls, the "race-through-the-day" mind-set takes hold and then further exacerbates one's upset at having to wait for anything.

The Benefits of Time-Shifting

When you find yourself waiting in lines, practice appropriate time-shifting to avoid crowds. Consider these suggestions:

➤ Buy your movie tickets early, take a walk, and then return three minutes before the picture starts (after everyone has already filed into the theater). There are always available seats, even for twosomes; theater management knows exactly how many tickets they're selling for each showing.

➤ Or, go to the theater early for the first showing, buy your tickets, go in and take a seat, and for the next 20 minutes or so listen to music with ear buds.

➤ If you commute, rather than going earlier or later, explore not going in at all—by telecommuting. (I'll discuss this in detail in Chapter 8, ("Sustaining Your Priorities for Fun and Profit").

➤ To avoid airlock, fly in the day before and fly out after everyone else has. Schedule travel time, particularly around Thanksgiving and Christmas, as much as six months in advance. You might stay home during those times and travel when everyone else is not—namely, the week after the holidays. More on this in Chapter 21, "Traveling Light—And Loving I"t

➤ To avoid camplock, patronize some of the less-traveled national and state parks. Some 200 national parks and thousands of state parks do not experience hordes of visitors.

➤ To avoid shoplock, make more purchases by catalog—but be careful of how and when you give out your name. Otherwise you'll be inundated by dozens of other catalog vendors.

Transmuting Commuting into Something Useful

As metro areas keep expanding, and as daily commuting becomes more trying, some people, but not a significant number, telecommute (see Chapter 1). Telecommuters complete much of their work away from the traditional office.

The benefits to you include reduced commuting time; reduced personal cost for travel, clothing, and food; flexible working hours; more time for dependents; and, likely, greater autonomy.

You can rack up significant time savings by telecommuting, as detailed below:

How Commuting Adds Up to Lost Time

Round-Trip Minutes/Day	Equivalent Hours/Year	Number of 40-Hour Weeks
40	160	4
60	240	6
80	320	8
100	400	10

Perhaps you can sell your employers on this idea. The benefits to them include potentially higher productivity; reduced office or plant costs; the ability to accommodate physically challenged employees; and the ability to motivate new employees with an attractive stay-at-home-and-get-paid option.

Coming to Terms

Telecommuting means working outside the office (that is, away from your employer's base of operations) and staying in touch with coworkers via electronics, such as a computer, a fax, a pager, and a phone. It can be done from your home, a hotel, a satellite office, or even your car.

Stockbrokers, consultants, writers, and even top-level executives are finding that telecommuting enables them to maintain—even increase—their overall productivity. Jobs such as computer programming, translating, software engineering, sales, and system analysis are well suited for telecommuting. Other professions, such as telemarketing, research, word processing, publishing, and architecture, also lend themselves to effective telecommuting.

Telecommuting Has Had a Marginal Impact

Still, despite everything, telecommuting has been employed only marginally. Some employees have been directed to telecommute; others have requested the option. Yet, in business and in government, most employees don't telecommute.

Even on a limited basis, telecommuting can provide you with many benefits beyond the time saved by not commuting. These include cost-savings, as well as the freedom to focus on projects, initiate conceptual thinking, and exercise more control over your environment. Check it out!

Taking Charge When You Shop

"Shop 'til you drop" is often too true for too many people. Why do it? The list in this section contains a host of tips you can use to budget your time more effectively and feel less stressed when shopping (in general, and during the holidays):

➤ First, don't wait until the last days or hours before picking up a crucial item.

➤ Avoid going to huge shopping malls if you can. Use the 800-numbers found in catalogs, or go online. Ask that your name be kept off the vendors' direct-mail lists. Receiving dozens of unwanted catalogs throughout the year diminishes your breathing space and contributes to landfills.

> **Pause!**
> Don't patronize stores that have one line for purchases and another line for pickup. You'll easily double your time in line. Such an arrangement is highly beneficial for the store, but not for you.

➤ Spend a few minutes at home or work contemplating what you are going to buy and for whom. Then draw up a list and bring it with you—this will help keep you focused and less prone to becoming overwhelmed once you're inside the stores.

➤ If you have to go to a super regional mall because of the choice or selections available, arrive near the opening or closing. Don't compete with the mad rush of shoppers during peak hours.

➤ Find a mall entrance that is less popular than the others. You're likely to find a parking space more easily.

➤ Reduce the strain of carrying large bundles by choosing smaller-sized gifts, such as jewelry, compact discs, cassettes, gloves, sunglasses, and so forth.

➤ Shop on Monday, Tuesday, or Wednesday evenings. Avoid weekend shopping!

➤ Give yourself frequent breaks while shopping. It's not a marathon event. There is no reason to make shopping for friends and loved ones anything but a joyful experience. Lighten up!

➤ Patronize establishments that have one long line, now used in banks or airports, where the person at the front of the line goes to the next available service attendant.

➤ If you find a gift that would please many of those on your gift list, such as chocolates or a book, buy multiple quantities in one transaction to reduce overall shopping time.

➤ When buying holiday gifts and cards, make your shopping count three and four times. Think: Is there someone having a wedding, birthday, or baby shower soon? It might mean doing a little more shopping now, but you'll avoid many more trips in the throes of January, February, and March.

➤ If you anticipate a long line, bring something that will help to make the time pass by more easily. This could be a bit of reading material, something to eat, a hand-gripper, or even a hand-held game.

➤ Vote with your feet. If a store consistently causes you to wait and has not figured out how to handle varying streams of customers throughout the day and week (because they've never plotted their own internal rush hours), decide to take your business elsewhere.

➤ Once you transport the packages home, take them to your table, desk or wherever you're going to complete the shopping trip—you still have to remove tags and stickers, file the invoices, wrap items, mail some of them, and store others.

➤ Designate one evening for greeting cards—if you send out cards, send them all out the same evening; then they're out of the way and en route.

The simple reality of today is that society will grow more complex every day for the rest of your life. Who merits the blame? As we'll see in the next chapter, nobody.

The Time Master Says

Engaging in activities, at times when the masses are not, has never been a more useful option. Become a contrarian!

CHAPTER 6

Slowing the Pace of the Rat Race

In This Chapter:

➤ Follow the basics
➤ Turn your challenge into a question
➤ Time and money are inextricably linked
➤ Relinquishing low-level choices

In this chapter you'll discover a variety of subtle techniques for slowing down the rapid effects of the culture all round you.

I often give speeches at annual conventions and conferences. No longer am I amazed at the ever-growing variety of professional associations that have not only been established, but that actually have thousands of members. For example, there is (whether you believe it or not) a National Association of Sewer Service Companies, a Cranial Academy, a Medieval Academy of America, a Society of Certified Kitchen and Bathroom Designers, a Society of Wine Educators, and even an International Concatenated (the spelling is correct) Order of Hoo-Hoo. Ho-ho!

More people, more groups, more information generated. Where's it all leading? One result is that the amount of information that competes for your time on a daily basis is on the rise—and taking a staggering toll. You might have an M.B.A. degree, you could have ten years of management experience under your belt, and you might have read every book on time management in creation. Nevertheless, you can't keep up. You are not alone—and you are probably not to blame.

Experiencing Time Pressure is not a Personal Failing

Feeling time-pressed today is not generally connected to how you were raised; it's not a question of where you went to school, where you live, your profession, or who you married. Even individuals who display high self-worth and high self-esteem often have too many concerns competing for their time and attention; they feel extreme time pressure. Even people who set goals—and do it well—frequently feel overwhelmed.

Pause!
What's rarely acknowledged is the impact that over-information has on your own sense of adequacy. More and more professionals feel inadequate, as if somehow they're supposed to be on top of it all.

If you accept that the dissipation of your career and personal time is probably not your fault, you're already well on the road to winning back your time.

Scoop Out What You Need

Suppose you were parched and the only source of water was a huge, heavy rain barrel. One way to quench your thirst would be to lift it up and try to gulp a few sips at a time. This feat would require impressive strength and balance, but why waste so much effort on such a difficult way to drink? If you take a small cup, stick it in the rain barrel, and extract a couple of ounces at a time, you could far more easily quench your thirst.

Now consider the daily information deluge. When you attempt to take in everything that's flung your way, the predictable response is that you drown in information (and still don't quench your thirst).

Coming to Terms
A deluge can be anything that over-whelms, such as a large amount of rain falling on an area, or a huge amount of information confronting a person.

Tackling new information—such as integrating another technology into your work routine, or assimilating other changes—is smoother when you employ the basics.

What are the basics?

1. Follow directions.
2. Take one step at a time.
3. Assess where you are every couple of steps.
4. After each assessment, having determined that you are on the right path, continue.

Information comes to you at a breakneck pace, and that pace will accelerate day after day for the rest of your life. How can you avoid being overwhelmed? Don't bite off more than you can chew; sometimes slowing down is the best response to "too much of too much" competing for your time and attention. Slow down so that you can figure out the best way to proceed.

Sit and Ponder, Slow Down and Win

Hereafter, begin practicing a new response when too much is thrown at you: take a momentary pause. Slowing down has its virtues!

Too often, the reflex to take action only exacerbates your time-pressure problems. I'll tackle this issue head-on in Part 6.

Reflect and Win

Trying to stay on top of it all ensures frustration. Nobody can keep on top of everything, nor is the attempt worthwhile. What you can do—and this is a lot—is make choices about where (and to what) you'll direct your time and attention.

A Formula for Slowing Down

Over-achievers Anonymous annually bestows the America's *Most Overworked Person Award*. One winner was described as the most extreme example of someone in a position of power who has the ability to choose if and how he is going to take care of himself, and yet challenges the limits of human endurance.

When interviewed by a major newspaper, the award winner said he wasn't proud of the title, and he knew that he needed to make some changes, but he didn't know where to begin.

Turn the Challenge into a Question

The solution to many dilemmas lies in taking the reverse of your situation and making a question out of it. Suppose you don't know how to slow down. Then ask yourself, "What would someone who evenly paces himself do in my situation?" If you're honest with yourself, by merely posing the question, you open yourself to a world of insights. I suggest writing it at the top of a blank piece of paper or screen to have plenty of room for all the self-generated solutions that you are going to record.

Even if you've been in overdrive for months, posing the question "What would a calm person do?" to yourself opens you up to intriguing insights. Answers could include:

- ➤   Do stretches in the morning.
- ➤   Allocate more tasks to staff.
- ➤   Brainstorm with my staff.
- ➤   Always have lunch with a friend.
- ➤   Concentrate on the most profitable activities.
- ➤   Take more frequent walks throughout the day.
- ➤   See a therapist.
- ➤   Schedule more vacation time into my calendar.

No More Deficit-Spending

Many people feel overwhelmed in handling debts and financial obligations. The bills arrive and need to be paid. Staying in a positive cash-flow position can start to feel like a full-time job in itself. Running a deficit budget, if you're stuck there, is a full-scale time thief.

Chances are you have some financial deficits. For decades, millions of Americans have accumulated personal debt via credit cards, loans, and other forms of financing.

Sustained deficit-spending eventually erodes your ability to prepare for the future and, worse, to capitalize on current opportunities. What's all this got to do with winning back your time? The more you owe, the more squelched you are!

"I owe, I owe, it's off to work I go."

You might have "learned" to consume way past your needs. How would it feel, however, if all your credit cards were paid off? How would it feel if you paid your monthly rent or mortgage several months in advance? How would it feel if your car loan was paid off? How would it feel if you were actually able to pay some of your utility bills for months down the road? For most people, it would feel wonderful. You'd feel in control of your time. I've experienced this first-hand, because I do it, and the time spent worrying is reduced to zip.

I know the arguments about losing the (minuscule) interest I could have earned on the money, but when I have a huge credit and nothing is due, I smile. So will you.

Control Your Checkbook

To reduce your personal financial deficits, place a moratorium on spending—regardless of what items entice you—until your credit cards are paid off. Let's not, however, confuse issues. In Chapter 3, "Time Flies Whether You Want It To Or Not," I discuss briefly the value of paying others to do those things that you don't like to do—it's a way of investing in your freedom. This is a theme I'll return to in detail in Chapter 9, "Buying Yourself Some Time." That's not what I'm talking about here. Learning to rein in your tendency for overspending is different from buying back the time you would otherwise have to spend on unnecessary chores you actively dislike.

Here are some useful exercises for controlling your checkbook, simplifying your financial life, and winning back a little time:

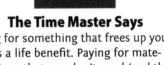

1. Pay bills in advance of their due dates.

2. Occasionally overpay the balance due on your continuing accounts, or pay early. This provides you the aforementioned psychological boost when you see a credit on your next statement, and it gives you a good reputation with your creditors—which could come in handy in the future.

The Time Master Says
Paying for something that frees up your time is a life benefit. Paying for material things that you don't need (and that certainly don't save you time) might be satisfying, but ultimately can be draining.

3. Considering forthcoming expenditures, which ones can you cut?

As author Roger Dawson says, it doesn't matter how much money you're making; if you're spending more than you take in each month, you're headed for trouble.

Beware: Choice Explosion beyond Practicality

One fundamental reason you might not be enjoying this time of your life as much as you did a year (or five years) ago is the number of choices you continually confront (one of the "mega-realities"). While flying from Denver to San Francisco and flipping through one of the airline magazines, I saw an ad for jelly beans. You remember jelly beans, little bundles of mouth-size fun? When people of my age were kids, how many different colors of jelly beans where there? Six, maybe eight? Let's see: green, black, pink, red, yellow, blue, and orange.

The ad I saw had names and pictures—if you can believe this—of 48 types of jelly beans. Peppermint polka-dot patty. Banana mint swirl. Lazy lime sublime. What's a kid to do?

It's not merely in the candy world that choices have proliferated. Visit a bike store, and the clerk asks you, "ten-speed, 15-speed, 21-speed, men's, women's, mountain bike, trail bike, or racing bike?" The same phenomenon occurs when you go to buy a tennis racquet, an exercise machine, a whirlpool bath, or even a birdbath (you have to shop for a birdbath to appreciate the overabundance of choices that can suddenly confront you. I wonder if all this choice matters to the birds.)

The New York Times ran a major feature saying that people are experiencing stress and anxiety today when shopping for leisure goods. There are so many choices! Weighing such choices takes up your time. The problem is worse in the workplace.

Reflect and Win

At all times, your goal is to scoop out information in amounts you can digest, and tackle activities in amounts you can do.

Pause!

At first blush, it would seem as if a plethora of choices is a good thing. After all, what can be the harm in having a wide variety of options available? The answer is that there is great harm in filling precious time with nagging-but-trivial decisions.

The Unrelenting Burden of Choosing

Consider the vendor product catalogs you're retaining. How about the flyers for management-training seminars? How about magazine and newsletter subscription offers at incredible savings? How about the coffee service options which await? In all directions, you're hit with more choices than you can reasonably ponder.

Every moment adds up. If you spend a lot of them contemplating which product or service to choose from among dozens or hundreds, you are consuming considerable amounts of your time. Once you choose, however wisely, it isn't once and for all. Next week, next month, next year, a new, better, faster, sleeker, less expensive, more powerful version of your product or service will be available. It will be that way for your whole life. (And many of these choices represent the small stuff. Chapter 18, "Decide or Let it Ride," focuses on making big decisions in record time.)

Your unrelenting chore to keep choosing is an unacknowledged aspect of being born into this culture at this time. And, once again, its cumulative effect is to rob you of your time.

As often as possible, avoid making such low-level choices. If the same yardstick is available in red, blue, yellow, or white, and it's all the same to you, grab the one that's closest—or take the one that the clerk hands you.

Whenever you find yourself having to make a low-level decision, consider this: Does this make a difference? Develop the habit of making only a few decisions a day: the ones that count. For the low-level issues, reclaim your right to say, "Who cares?" or "It doesn't matter."

You're in Control of Your Time and Your Decision

Some people proceed through their days and their lives as if others were in control of their time. How about you? Review this list and put a check mark next to any party on the list that you believe is in control of your time.

☐ Your parents?	☐ Spouse?
☐ Children?	☐ Neighbors?
☐ Community?	☐ Landlord or mortgagor?
☐ Company president?	☐ Boss?
☐ Coworkers?	☐ Peers?
☐ Industry?	☐ Opinion leaders?
☐ Government?	☐ Friends?
☐ The president?	☐ The "politically correct?"
☐ Governor, mayor?	☐ The press?
☐ Television, radio?	☐ Unknown forces?

When I ask people in seminars to complete this checklist, most catch on quickly and leave all the boxes unchecked. The one box that is checked, if any, is "Boss." There are bad bosses, unreasonable bosses, workaholic bosses, and even psychotic bosses. I've had them all! (See the section on "Managing Your Boss," in Chapter 11, "Loaning Yourself Out Less and Being Happier Because of It.") Your boss might pile on the assignments, but you're the one who determines how, largely when, and often with whom you'll tackle them.

Pause!

Family and friends are important but their expectations should not dictate how you spend your time. "Being there" for them is not the same thing as being at their beck and call.

If you believe your boss or anyone else ultimately controls your time, you'll have to struggle to win back your time.

Be Your Own Consultant

Perhaps you have no problem acknowledging intellectually that you are, in fact, in control of your time. Putting that knowledge into practice might be a bit more difficult. An article I once read taught me a technique for proceeding when confronted with too much stuff competing for my time and attention. It originated with none other than Richard Nixon, America's 37th president. Nixon practiced the notion of becoming a consultant to himself.

When you're faced with many choices (what decision to make, which road to take, which dish to bake), pretend that you are a highly paid consultant—to yourself. If your last name is Smith, your internal dialogue would begin as follows: "What does Smith need to do next?" You proceed as if separating yourself from your physical shell, moving to a corner of the room and observing your body from the vantage point of an objective third party.

By referring to yourself in the third person ("What does Smith need to do next?"), you derive different answers from those you'd derive if you thought, "What should I do next?"

How so? A semantic shift occurs when you refer to yourself as if you were an observer. A channel of discovery opens that is not readily available to you otherwise. (Maybe it has to do with whether you're seeing the forest or the trees.)

When can you use this technique? When can't you use it? Becoming a consultant to oneself works as well in crunch times as it does in milder times. A variation on this theme is to pretend a real-life trusted advisor or mentor is there with you. Ask yourself how he or she would advise you.

If you have, say, six tasks facing you, no faster or more efficient way exists than identifying the most important one, tackling it, then continuing to number two. In the long run, any other method for proceeding, however psychologically satisfying, cannot compete with tackling the tasks in order of the importance you've assigned them.

Exhibit Your Inner Wisdom

Whether it's becoming a contrarian, taking one step at a time, spending less and keeping your debts to zero, being more prudent about the information you ingest, remembering who's in control, avoiding low-level choices when possible, or becoming a consultant to yourself, you can always turn to yourself for the important task of safeguarding your time.

The Time Master Says

You are more resourceful than you often acknowledge, and you always have more options than you know.

PART 2

Appointing Yourself in Charge

Part 2
Appointing Yourself in Charge

Armed with all the insights you gained in Part 1, let's now focus on identifying and pursuing your priorities. Then we'll move on to why time and money are not the same thing, and to an eye-opening look at why you're hardly able to stay awake during the day and then (too often) find yourself up all night.

When you're well-rested, you can better handle whatever others—your boss, family, friends, and neighbors—ask you to do, hence, the more capable you are to them!

CHAPTER 7

What Matters Most to You?

In This Chapter:

➤ Choose and support only a handful of priorities

➤ Health, wealth, and wisdom accumulate gradually

➤ Reinforce your priorities, support your goals

In this chapter we'll explore the importance of priorities and goals and how to ensure that we spend our time in accordance with what we've identified to be important.

What do we want for ourselves? The powers that be on Madison Avenue and in Hollywood have gotten so good at manipulating us all that the wants and needs that we genuinely believe were self-generated, for the most part, come from carefully-crafted campaigns that command our attention, stoke our emotions, and stimulate the deep well of desire within each of us.

Wants and Desires as Corporate Creations

In his classic book *Culture Jamming*, author Kalle Lasn says, "American culture is no longer created by the people. Our stories, once passed from one generation to the next by parents, neighbors and teachers, are now told by distant corporations with 'something to sell as well as to tell.'"

If you don't . . . or can't . . . decide what's important to you, almost anything can (and will) compete for your time and attention—and thereby dissipate your day, your week, your year, your career, and your life. Once you decide what's important to you, you can then become a consultant to yourself to determine what it actually takes to maintain or achieve what you've designated as important.

Reflect and Win

In *Flow: The Psychology of Optimal Experience,* Mihaly Csikszentmihalyi says, "There is no inherent problem in our desire to escalate our goals, as long as we enjoy the struggle along the way."

Knowing what you want means being honest with yourself. It also means taking the time and trouble to list priorities and review your list often until they sink in. You've encountered this type of advice before, but did you follow it?

The Key Priorities in Life (for Most People)

The Time Master Says
If you don't know where you're going, any road will take you there.

The great paradox about priorities is that if you have too many then, logically, they can't all be priorities. Do you have 18 items that you list as top priorities in your life? If so, reconsider, because no one can pay homage to 18 top priorities.

To help you identify your priorities, let's examine the concerns that traditionally have served as top priorities for many people. Not that your list has to match this one—it probably won't—but this is a starting point:

Coming to Terms
A paradox is a situation where contradictory statements could both be true, as evident in the question "If you accept that God is all powerful, can he make a rock so big that even he can't lift it?"

➤ Family
➤ Society
➤ Health and well-being

➤   Wealth
➤   Career growth
➤   Intellectual growth
➤   Spiritual growth

Keep in mind that you might have others, not listed here, that are appropriate for you.

Family Values

For most people, the family is #1. If you're married and you love your spouse, being with your spouse is easily a top priority. If you have children and you love them, it's the same situation. If you're single, your priority might be to find a spouse and to raise a family, or to treat the people closest to you like a chosen family. If you're in school, it might be to spend time with your nuclear family: your mom and dad, your brothers and sisters.

Reflect and Win

As with all the priorities to be discussed, to attach goals—specific, action-oriented steps with timelines—to your priorities to reinforce them. Write them down.

If family is a top priority, then one of your goals might be to earnestly listen to your spouse for at least 15 minutes three times per week. (Won't he or she be pleased if you listen at all!)

Likewise, you can choose a variety of other goals to support this priority. Here is a quick list of other possible goals related to family:

➤   Take the children for a day-trip once every three weeks.
➤   Have a photo of the family taken every other December, as a shared family project every year.
➤   Have or adopt one or more children within seven years. (Many kids need good homes.)
➤   Send flowers to your spouse, unannounced, once a month.
➤   Buy life insurance to ensure your family's prosperity in the event of your demise. (Maybe you'd better not announce this one.)

Many of the goals that support your family priority are related to other priorities, such as wealth, intellectual growth, and so forth. It's wonderfully efficient when you set goals that address more than one priority.

Community Spirit: Getting Involved

If you want to do something about society's woes (besides yell at your TV set), participate in your community. You might become involved with religious, social, fraternal, or community groups. You might choose to run for local office—not for purposes of ego gratification, but to give something of value back to the community. Here are some possible activities that might support your social priorities:

➤ Volunteer to serve on the Welcome Wagon Committee for new residents.
➤ Contribute to the XYZ campaign in the forthcoming election.
➤ Begin an environmental-awareness movement in your town by April 1.
➤ Recycle your paper, plastic, and glass every week hereafter.
➤ Run for town council for the next term.
➤ Write an article by August 31 on the importance of nurturing America's youth.
➤ Be the host to a foreign exchange student during the next academic year.
➤ Chair this season's March of Dimes campaign in your region, or volunteer on a Habitat for Humanity project.
➤ Coach a community-league sports team.
➤ Volunteer a week of each month at a local homeless shelter or kitchen.
➤ Tutor a student from your local elementary or high school.
➤ Participate in a community theater or choral production.

Yes, it takes time and energy to support your priorities. Hold that thought. If your goal is to win back your time, why would you want suggestions for new stuff that you're not currently undertaking? The answer: tasks in support of your priorities help you win back your time, and it's less of a mystery than it might seem.

The Time Master Says
The few things that you'll do in support of your priorities will take less time than all the things you do now in support of who-knows-what. And they'll have the added benefit of moving you closer to your goals. That's time well spent!

Identifying your priorities and establishing some goals to support those priorities is inherently efficient.

To Your Health

Some people think that they can shortchange sleep, nutrition, or other vital aspects of health and still be at their best. In the short term, you can make do in a crunch period and sometimes proceed with less than the best rest and nutrition. If this becomes a long-term phenomenon, however, you're doing a disservice to yourself, your employer, and probably your family and friends. Carve out 15 or 20 minutes on some Saturday or Sunday morning to take stock of your life and the fundamental resources you need to be at your best.

Do you need more sleep? Probably so.

Do you need better nutrition? For many people the answer is yes.

Do you need to see a masseuse? Ah, the wonders!

Do you need to join a health club?

Do you need to sit in a steam bath?

While I eschew multitasking, I do believe in achieving two-for-one payoffs when it is practical. If you attempt to carve out time for exercise and time to, say, watch TV with your kids, you could be stretched to the limits. A better alternative would be to engage in exercise with your kids. Take a soccer ball out to the field, go biking, swim together, or do anything that helps condition your heart and lungs while being together. Having a meal together is certainly also worthwhile, but, these days, many American families rarely do.

Pause!

In general, watching television is simply being alone together. Watching television together can be okay if you discuss what you are watching during or after the program. Alternatively, maybe you have a favorite table game or two that you haven't played in a while.

Seek to engage in some type of group exercise such as walking together to the store, taking a hike along a trail, or simply walking to a neighbor's house. If you live in a house with a yard, turn yard work into fun.

Get Fit, Stay Fit

If you believe you don't have time to work out, think again. The time you invest in exercising more than pays off in mental alertness, creativity, and productivity.

Suppose you used to work out for thirty minutes every second or third day. You might think that those ninety minutes every week is time you can't afford to spend. Yet, if you let week after week go by without working out, you are not as sharp at work, you tend to be a little drowsy, and your productivity can suffer. We all know people who barely make it to the end of the day; they watch the clock for the last hour or so. At home, they engage in energy-draining activities such as sitting in a chair with a remote control or a mouse.

Reflect and Win

Energy begets energy. Stand up and walk. You've got a long journey both in terms of your career and your life. With decades to go, you don't want to let yourself become a potato puff.

Obesity is on the rise. Problems soon follow. This doesn't have to be your fate. You have the capability to make the most of your time by working out on a regular basis, and hence being at your best more of the time.

Pause!

Check with your doctor before you start any exercise or diet program, especially if you haven't been exerting yourself much. You'll receive valuable (maybe life-saving) guidance.

Here are dozens of activities in support of your health and well-being priorities.

➤ Join a health club within a month and set a goal of working out four times per week for at least 30 minutes.
➤ Buy five healthy foods you've never tried.
➤ Take two health-and-fitness books out of the library, read them cover to cover, and gain at least five new ideas you'll put into practice within one month.
➤ Become a lifetime member of a local bicycle club, walking club, or exercise group.
➤ Begin going on walking and hiking dates rather than going to restaurants and movies.
➤ Hire a fitness trainer in February.
➤ Have an annual check-up every January (especially important if you live alone and don't cook).
➤ Take daily vitamin supplements that meet your needs, as determined by a dietitian.
➤ Ingest 50 percent less alcohol per week, starting this week.
➤ Make one weekend hike of at least 6 miles every weekend.
➤ Visit a dietitian this month to determine your nutritional needs.

Having well-being as a priority gives you a license to behave in new ways. Picking up a piece of litter in a neighbor's yard, for example, is good for you, is good for the neighbor, and the community.

Money Matters

Accumulating wealth is not evil. The *Bible* says "the love of money is the root of all evil." It doesn't say that money per se is the root of all evil. You can accumulate buckets of money, as long as you don't love your money more than people or yourself.

Wealth comes in many forms: intellectual, spiritual, and so forth, to be covered in subsequent pages. Let's focus here on economic wealth. Here are examples of goals you could choose in support of this priority:

➤ I will call a certified financial planner this month and pay him or her to advise me about how to invest for the future.
➤ I will start an IRA this Tuesday and contribute x amount of dollars each month until I reach the maximum contribution level.
➤ This week, I will redirect my employer to automatically invest x amount from my paycheck in a 401(k), mutual fund account, or other investment.
➤ By next quarter, I will lower the number of deductions on my paycheck so I receive a larger refund from the IRS after filing taxes at the end of this year.
➤ I will join an investment club this month, meet with the members monthly, learn about investment opportunities, and participate in intelligently selected group investments.

➤   (For sales professionals) I will earn $x in commissions for the fourth quarter of 201X.

➤   By September 30, 201X, I will launch the business venture of my dreams.

➤   This month, I will trim monthly expenditures by $400.

➤   Within six months, I will live within my means.

➤   I will open a retirement account with my credit union next week.

➤   I will bring my lunch to work at least three times per week.

➤   I will choose an automobile that achieves better gas mileage.

For most people, amassing wealth is a long-term affair. Only a tiny fraction of the population ever wins the lottery. (The odds of being struck by lightning are greater.)

You add to your net worth a little at a time. Gradually, inexorably, the wealth begins to build. *Fortune* and *Forbes* articles on wealthy Americans reveal that the majority got wealthy slowly. The book *The Millionaire Next Door* confirms that wealthy people developed a habit, early on, of living within their means—and one day found their nest egg had grown to a sizable sum. Wow, what a way to win back your time—by developing habits of wealth, breaking the cycle of deficit-spending, and amassing a sum that lets you to do what you want in life!

The Time Master Says
Wealth, like happiness and fitness, is a habit. You become wealthy by developing habits of wealth. If you're on your way to wealth, it's probably your habits.

Your Brilliant Career

Beyond what's already been discussed, the pursuit of career growth, per se, might be one of your priorities. If you've invested years in rising to where you are, and if you like what you do, rising within your industry or profession is predictable.

Independent of the monetary rewards, those who are highly learned and well-respected in their chosen fields enjoy a high level of inner satisfaction. Here are possible goals in support of your career-growth priority:

➤   Read one new book a month by the top authors writing in your field.

➤   Subscribe to (or start reading in your company library) two important industry publications you don't currently receive.

➤   Form a monthly study group so that you all encourage each other in learning more about your chosen fields.

➤   Register this week to attend a forthcoming conference (or submit a proposal to make a presentation of your own there).

➤ Return to school to earn a graduate degree in your field.
➤ Undertake original research over the next six months, put your findings into article from, and pursue having it published in a prominent industry journal.
➤ Complete the certification process in your industry by December 31, 201X.
➤ Volunteer for that special task force forming in April.
➤ Join your professional association, or (if you're already a member) run for office in it.

As society grows more complex (and, by now, you know it will), you will benefit by becoming more of a specialist in your chosen field. The typical business manager reads as much as four hours a day, be it from books, magazines, documents, reports, the web, email, and so on. When it come to career-related reading the trick, for most professionals, is to be more focused. One caveat: it pays to specialize only if you know your specialty is marketable and has long-term prospects. If you're worried that becoming too specialized will restrict your intellectual diversity, fear not. Once you decide on pursuing a highly narrow field, it actually expands. You begin to see things within your narrow focus that you couldn't have seen before making the choice.

Reflect and Win

The more specialized you become, the more potentially valuable you become to those who need your expertise.

Thinking Your Way to Intellectual Growth

When Supreme Court Justice Oliver Wendell Holmes was in his 90s (quite aged for his day), he was asked why he was reading the voluminous book *Plato*. He responded, "To improve my mind."

Rumor has it that the pursuit of intellectual growth—independent of career growth—is a worthy priority. Certainly education and intellectual development—for its own sake, and for that of your children—rank at the top of any list of priorities you might devise. In support of this priority, here's a smorgasbord of possible goals:

➤ Read one new book every month that is not in your field or connected to what you do for a living.
➤ Spend time with your children playing games such as Scrabble to help develop their vocabulary and love of words.
➤ Enroll in a local community college course that interests you.

➤ Take at least one international trip per year to a destination completely foreign and learn firsthand about other cultures.

➤ Sign up for the lecture series sponsored by the local Chamber of Commerce so you can hear from visiting authorities on contemporary issues.

➤ Watch at least one program per week on The Learning Channel or PBS.

➤ View a documentary rather than a feature film.

➤ Read a historical account instead of a mystery.

More worthy and stimulating issues compete for your time and attention than you will ever be able to pursue. Staying primarily with a few pre-identified focus areas takes strength while, of course, occasionally allowing yourself to freewheel all over creation. (You are, after all, only human, aren't you?)

Pause!

As with life priorities, devise some parameters before sitting down and simply freewheeling on the web. Otherwise, rather than winning back your time, you'll watch it dissipate among an infinite number of seemingly intellectual pursuits.

Nurturing the Great Spirit Within

Some folks are sensitive about religion, sometimes taking offense where none is intended. Spiritual growth doesn't mean going to a place of worship each week, although it certainly could involve that. Your spiritual growth can occur anywhere, at any time. If you seek active spiritual growth as a priority, these goals support your choice:

➤ Take weekly walks in natural settings and appreciate your surroundings.

➤ Actually read the holy book for your religion during the next calendar year, or listen to a recording of it.

➤ Live as if every creature on earth is a divine creation. You can start this anytime, and it never ends.

➤ Practice the art of forgiveness by making three calls this week to people you need to forgive. ("Do I have to?" Only if you're serious about your well-being.)

➤ Give thanks each morning or evening for all you have been given in life.

➤ Decide to regularly attend weekly religious services.

➤ Donate your time and energy monthly to a food shelter for the needy.

➤ Scour your home this week to find everything you can donate to others.

➤ Listen to inspirational music.

➤ Pray for yourself and others.

Now then, that's seven possible priority areas thus far—and even they're not the be-all and end-all. You might have some that don't fit within these categories. That's fine, as long as you choose goals that involve specific action steps and time lines in support of your priorities.

Your Actions Speak Louder than Your Words

To support the priorities you choose, here are some action steps:

➤ Write down everything that's important to you or that you want to accomplish in your life. A long list is okay.

➤ Several days later, re-examine the list. Cross out anything that no longer strikes your fancy. Feel free to add a few things if they come up.

➤ Another day, review your list and see whether any items can be grouped together. Then, reword or re-label those choices. Feel free to drop items.

➤ Put your list away for yet another day. (Yes, this is going to take a week!) Then review it again.

➤ Once more, combine, regroup, or delete things on the list as seems appropriate.

➤ Prepare the final draft of your list, recognizing that in time it might change. For now, these are what you've identified as your priorities.

Print your list in a reduced point size (or simply hand-print it in miniature) so that it's small enough to carry in your wallet or purse. Then review your list of priorities at least once a day. With so many other things competing for your time and attention, it's easy to lose sight of your priorities by 10:00 in the morning. It's not excessive to read your priority list several times a day.

The Time Master Says

Some of the most accomplished people, who routinely appear to be in great control of their time, review their priority lists often.

CHAPTER 8

Sustaining Your Priorities for Fun and Profit

In This Chapter:

➤ Your unspoken commitments
➤ Supporting your priorities with goals you'll implement
➤ Signs that you're heading off course
➤ Managing your to-do list and balancing short-term and long-term tasks

In this chapter, you'll learn how to reinforce your commitment to your newly established priorities, and discover ways to quickly recognize when you've derailed your progress toward achieving them.

The Value of Wanting What You Have

In the mid-1960s song of the same name, singer Peggy Lee rhetorically asked about life, "Is that all there is?" Often, life doesn't meet our expectations. As a struggling young actor, Clint Eastwood worked hard to become successful. When he became an international box office star and experienced worldwide adulation, he told a reporter how he was surprised that he didn't feel overjoyed and satisfied with his success.

Some people fear the consequences of success, a la, "Be careful of what you wish for, because you might get it," and if so, then what would you do? It is vital to ask yourself, "Do I actually want this? Do I want it so badly that I will accept the detriments along with the benefits?" In other words, imagine you've already realized your pursuit. Then, ask yourself, "Am I where I want to be?"

Some people maintain unspoken commitments, such as those listed below—behaviors and activities that predominate even over carefully chosen priorities.

What Are Your Unspoken Commitments?

☐ To be needed or accepted?
☐ To over-file, or over-collect?
☐ To wait for permission?
☐ To hold back?
☐ To repeatedly push yourself to your productive limit?
☐ To withhold your emotions?
☐ To be easily intimidated by the experience or status of others?
☐ To dress down?
☐ To spend money as soon as it comes in?

Suppose you identify your priorities and establish some goals in support of them. What will it take to *ensure* that you stay on your chosen path? Desire and focus. If you know what you want, but can't maintain a clear focus, the odds of being successful diminish markedly.

Alas, focus seems to be such a rare commodity these days. It's easy to stray—agreed? If you had a nickel for every time you heard somebody decide to do something and then saw them do little or nothing in support of the decision, you'd probably be rich!

Building in Positive Reinforcements

Keeping on track with your priorities means staying focused. Daily, you can make it easier for yourself if you develop positive reinforcements. Here are reinforcement techniques to use in support of the priorities you've chosen:

➤ Join others who have priorities and goals similar to yours—and who are supporting them. Perhaps there is a professional or social organization that fits the bill.
➤ Surround yourself with reinforcing statements, reminders, and self-stick notes so you don't lose sight of what you have already deemed important.
➤ Record affirmations of your priorities and supporting goals such as: "I choose to visit the health club four times a week for a minimum workout of 30 minutes."
➤ Prepare a budget to help determine exactly the cost to honor your priorities and the goals you've chosen to support them.
➤ Develop supporting rituals. If your goal is to lose 6 pounds by the end of June, begin taking the stairs instead of the elevator whenever you're heading down for lunch or to your car at the end of the day.

➤ Keep your action steps bite-size. Choosing goals that are too difficult to achieve offers little value in honoring the associated priority.

➤ Report to someone. Having some significant other serving as a coach or supporter ensures that you do what you said you would. (High achievers do this!)

➤ Visualize the goal every day—Olympic athletes aboard a plane, can experience improved performance once they land if they visualize during the flight.

➤ Offer yourself small rewards when you behave in ways that support your quest.

If this works for you, contract with yourself! Author Dennis Hensley describes advancement by contract: "A contract takes precedence over everything else. For example, you make your monthly house payment rather than using the money for a vacation because you have to make that payment: The contract allows the bank to repossess your home if you do not fulfill your obligation."

He suggests carefully selecting three to five major goals (in support of your priorities) and then signing a contract that aids you in reaching them. "Once under contract, you would have to succeed by a selected date or else face the consequences of defaulting on the contract." Make three copies of your contract. Keep the original. Give one copy each to your spouse, a trusted coworker, and a friend.

SELF-INITIATED CONTRACT

I, _____, agree to accomplish each of the following items on or before _____ and hereby do formally contract myself to these purposes.

These goals are challenging but reasonable, and I accept them willingly.

A. _____

B. _____

C. _____

Signature: _____ *Date:* _____

Review your contract when you find yourself becoming distracted by small details or if you think you are not moving in the right direction.

Another wonderful strategy is to plot your campaign on a calendar. Start from the ending date (the deadline for completing your goal) and work back to the present, plotting the subtasks and activities you'll need to undertake.

Proceeding in reverse through the monthly calendar helps you establish realistic interim dates that reflect not only your available resources, but also vacations, holidays, weekends, other off-duty hours, and reasonable output levels. Start with a major deadline, then work backward to set realistic interim dates for achieving what you want.

Coming to Terms

When something is interim it is temporary or transitional.

The Time Master Says

Give yourself flexibility; build in some downtime, vacation time, and so forth. Devise a realistic plan to accomplish your goal by the time you said you would.

Straying, or Staying On Course?

On more than one occasion you're bound to go off course. When you do, revisit the list of reinforcement strategies above, and engage another.

Here are some warning signs that you're off the path you chose:

➤   You've talked a good game, and that's all. You said that something is important to you, but you haven't scheduled any time or allocated any funds for it.

➤   You stated that working out four times a week was important; by the third week, you're making excuses to yourself about why you're not.

➤   You've let piles of paper stack up. Although you've chosen only a handful of priorities, you find yourself wading through stuff that's interesting and not important.

➤   Your goals miss the mark. Despite the toil, time, and thought you put into establishing your goals, it's apparent they're not supporting your priorities.

Long-Term Versus Short-Term Tasks

It's likely you face an age-old dilemma: staying on top of all the things you need or want to accomplish.

Reflect and Win

If you haven't yet considered using the super-long to-do strategy, give it a try. Your first super-long list will probably fill two to five pages—it should be easy to move items up to the front as needed. You'll have a clear idea of what you face all on one big roster, and you'll keep your priorities sharp for years to come.

People are always asking me about to-do lists. Do they need to maintain them? How can they go about fixing them? Everyone in the work-a-day world uses some kind of list as a tool for getting things done. I'm neither for nor opposed to any system you employ to stay efficient; judge by your results. (Chapter 14, "Top Time-Management Tools Revealed," explores some time-management tools and technologies.)

If you maintain some type of to-do list, you can use it to support your priorities by lengthening it for strategic reasons, without overloading yourself. Read on.

Balancing Short-term and Long-term Tasks

Balancing short-term against long-term tasks and activities is not easy. For years, I maintained an eight-page to-do list! I had hundreds of things on my to-do list, arranged by major life priorities. Most items on the list were medium- to long-range activities.

The first page of my list represented only the short-term activities—those I had chosen to do now or this week. I drew continually from the eight-page list, moving items to the top as it became desirable (or necessary) to tackle them.

In essence, I maintained a dynamic to-do list; it contained everything I wanted to achieve, but always with only one page I needed to look at: the top page. Yes, I was forever updating the list and printing out new versions, but so many advantages exist that I wouldn't think of doing it any other way.

I'd review the entire list periodically, always moving items from, say, page 7 up to the front page. Thus, any anxiety stays at a rather low level.

Managing Long-term or Repeated Tasks

Maintaining a long to-do list helped me become more proficient in managing long-term or repeated tasks. If I was working on a long-term project, I could continually draw from it those portions that could be handled in the short-term; I moved them up to the front page. Likewise, if a task was a repeat or cyclical project—something I had to do every month or every year—I could choose a portion of the task and move into the short-term (up to the front page).

On occasion, you can short-circuit the to-do list and complete tasks without even entering them on your list. Rather than adding it to your to-do list, try a fast-action option: record your letters and fire them off in an email or text message.

Goals: Setting Them and Reaching Them

Subdivide your goals into smaller chunks and assign a time frame to each. Software to help you stay on track and in control of your time has improved markedly in the last few years.

With scheduling and time management software and tools, the ever-present caveat is that the software can only be as good as your last update. If you don't maintain the system by consistently logging in your latest appointment, your project notes, and any other updates or modifications to the tasks and activities before you, then the software will not serve you.

Until such systems encompass artificial intelligence which includes a 1) camera or seeing eye, 2) an optical scanner, 3) voice recognition capabilities, and 4) a mechanical arm that literally moves items about on your desk, you will have to do the work of keeping your data up to date.

One day, we might all don headbands that capture our brain waves and transmit the signals to the software. On that hallowed day, you can simply "direct your thoughts" into your computer which will file, maintain, update your data, and offer your notes, reminders, report forms, logs,

Reflect and Win

You are the driving force that spells the difference between whether these tools will have high utility for you or they merely become another daily burden.

Pause!

Remember, all time management tools, be they software, pocket organizers, or hard copy systems, will let you down the moment you don't keep them up. None of them operates by magic. They all require your continual and vital input.

and schedules when you "mentally" request them. Until then, choose your update method carefully.

A New Generation of Apps

Employ scheduling, time management, or project management apps if this supports the way you work. Many popular programs are available and the learning curve is such that you can master most components of them within a day or two. Chances are you'll become a fairly proficient user within a matter of weeks.

Whether you use software or simply plot out your progress on a wall chart, the way that you proceed is relatively the same. You identify what needs to be done first, second, and so on, post it, proceed towards its accomplishment, plot your progress, and constantly review where you are and where you're heading. You revise your chart as necessary, and remember to reward yourself along the way when you have accomplished something.

Updating Your System Pays Off

When you update a time management app (scheduling appointments, putting in key phone numbers and so forth), or when you update a contact management app (entering the phone, e-mail address and web site of key contacts), magic begins to happen. As you have less scraps of paper in and around your desk visually competing for your attention, you also begin to have a clearer focus, more direction, and sometimes, even more energy to face the day.

The Time Master Says

Apps can do great things: A scheduler lets you know when it's time to make a call. ID status components enable you to file away contacts by industry, geography, or what have you. You can retrieve vital info with a few key strokes.

When is the last time you've taken several days or even several hours to give such powerful programs your full and undivided attention?

Reflect and Win

Even if you think you have too much to do, clear away time to better learn to use tools that would greatly enhance your use of time in the long run, so that you wouldn't be caught in a catch-22 to begin with.

Break out of the box now and, whether it's consuming one Saturday morning or staying at work late one Wednesday evening, focus intently on apps you already have available.

Old Standbys: Paper and Pencil

If you already suffer from too much technology, a simple system that will keep you on top of the goals that support your priorities works surprisingly well. Acquire a washable wall chart or an oversized set of monthly calendars. Mount your calendars on the wall and use magic markers, washable felt-tip pens, sticky-note pads, gold stars, red seals, or what have you to represent what you want to accomplish by when. This isn't news to you if you work in an office where any number of people, vehicles, or goods, need to be scheduled for optimum efficiency.

On a personal basis, such calendar plotting works well; you're the boss of the calendar. Moving self-stick notes around is a one-second maneuver. High-tech or low-tech, do what works.

At all times, use the tools that comfort you. Watch out that you don't re-clutter your immediate environment. In other words, use only the paper tools and supplies that support your efforts.

CHAPTER 9

Buying Yourself Some Time

In This Chapter:

➤ Doing too much yourself is not a good idea
➤ You can always make more money;
   you can't make more time
➤ Splurge for services on occasion
➤ Helpers can handle many things for you.

This chapter explains why getting help with professional and personal tasks might be the best move you can make to win back your time.

Some time management gurus suggest that you record how you spend each hour of the day for one week or one month. Then, like doing a budget, you see the number of hours you've wasted, and, like money wasted, you wish you had those hours back.

Make a time diary if you wish, but I don't think it's necessary. Human nature being what it is, you're going to continue to hang on to some tasks, even those you know ought to be delegated to others or dropped all together. Relax, it's not a death knell to hang on to some things.

Reflect and Win

Start delegating, casting off, or otherwise eliminating low-level items from your to-do list all together. Each time you remove some unnecessary task from your schedule, you gain time to tackle more vitals tasks that will yield far greater results.

The Dangers of Taking on Too Much

In the work-a-day world, you encounter middle managers seeking to leapfrog several positions in an organization by taking on more tasks and responsibilities, although they're already working beyond optimal capacity. Among entrepreneurs, you might encounter someone trying to crack a new market—even while juggling several other balls, short-changing his or her health to keep that circus going.

What are danger signs that you believe you have to "do it all" yourself? Consider these symptoms: You think you'll be able to overcome obstacles by working longer; you tell yourself (or worse, your boss) that you "appreciate the challenge." If people around you think it can't be done, all the better; you'll wow 'em by doing the impossible; right?

You might become a little overbearing, but, hey, you're in pursuit of an important goal and that's what counts. Besides, you're the "only one who can do the job."

Pause!
Beware if you start believing that you alone are the only one who can handle things. Many organizations seek out people with such urges. "Only superheroes need apply."

Working hard per se is not a problem, unless you maintain preposterous ambitions or let force of habit push you beyond the point of diminishing returns. Too many career achievers fall into an endless cycle. These people feel their accomplishments are too small or too few; they experience disappointment, frustration, and health-threatening stress. To relieve these feelings, they work harder in the hope they'll accomplish more and a golden rainbow will appear.

"Doing it All" is Costly

If you think working extremely hard is the only way to gain the respect of others—or self-respect—rethink your approach.

Some do-it-all people maintain the notion that the only way to exhibit

Reflect and Win
Contemplate using help for selected segments of your life. Admit to yourself that you can't do everything; acknowledge that trying harder, sometimes, might not be worth it.

competence is by constantly demonstrating it to everyone else. Worse, if they never quite prove it to themselves, they live in dread of being found out as imperfect.

➤ Rather than focus on your weaknesses, accentuate the positive! Develop your strengths. Also give yourself realistic time frames for ambitious goals.

➤ Divide and conquer. Take smaller steps when setting larger goals so that you don't burst a spleen in progress. When progress is slow, seek an alternate route, a new door, or a different mind-set: anything but plodding along the same as always.

Delegate and Win

Especially when it comes to domestic tasks, do you become stuck playing small? Do you think that if you spend a few minutes on the fly, taking care of this and that, you can handle all you seek to accomplish—and avoid spending money to have others help? Many people do.

Each time you avoid hiring a service professional, helper, or part-timer—when such parties could aid you considerably—you ensure that you won't win back your time. Each time you mow the grass, for example, when you don't enjoy doing it, you add to the cumulative total of undesirable tasks in your life.

Time Is Short; Money Is Replenishable

Invariably someone asks, "What do I do if money is tight?" I don't presume that you have trunk loads of cash stashed away somewhere. And the thought of parting with some of your money to hire people to do what you've traditionally done yourself might seem like heresy at first.

The Time Master Says
It makes sense to pay a high-school student $15 to mow the lawn if you can't stand doing so. In the long run, you won't miss the money and you'll be glad you're no longer mowing the lawn.

What is the time value, however, of the money you might part with to have a mundane chore completed? Do you want to trade a few dollars to have tasks accomplished and free up some of your time? (Hint: The answer is three letters long.)

Consider the act of hiring others, from the vantage point of your life's big picture. You have things to accomplish that can perhaps make you much more money than the $15 you pay somebody to mow the lawn or trim the hedges.

If you're an entrepreneur or self-employed, it pays to rely on outside services so you can focus on what you do best and make the overall business prosper. If you work for an organization, countless opportunities for relief are available; you can rely on others (at work and away from work) to alleviate the piddling tasks you don't enjoy doing. Thus, you can be at your best and be noticed by superiors. You stand a better chance of receiving those raises and promotions.

Coming to Terms

Piddling means paltry, trivial, or inconsequential.

When Not Doing It All Works Wonders

It's surprising how common the do-it-all urge is. Nanci Hellmich, a reporter for *USA Today*, uncovered this when she interviewed me for two articles. The first was a brief, two-column article; in it, Nanci invited readers to write to *USA Today* and discuss their time-pressure problems. Several readers would benefit from my counsel (aw, shucks). The second article would include the results of my counseling.

Over several weeks, Nanci received hundreds of letters; she selected respondents for me to call. I lived in Falls Church, Virginia at the time, and I made the calls from the *USA Today* offices in Arlington, Virginia. I had involved conversations with a female attorney and a graduate student, among others.

The attorney was constantly racing the clock, taking her daughters to school in the morning, seeing her husband off on his (frequently long) business trips, plying her trade as a partner in a successful law firm, picking up the children, driving them to various after-school activities, making dinner, reading to them, and putting them to bed.

After listening to her story, I suggested that she order dinner a couple of times a week rather than making it all the time. She said she'd never thought about it, and it seemed a little extravagant. I asked her how much she earned. It was considerable. I asked her how much her husband earned. It was more than considerable.

"Okay," I replied, "between the two of you, you're clearing nearly $350,000 per year. Suppose you occasionally had Chinese food, pizza, or chicken delivered to your home. Weekly, how much would it cost for dinner delivered?" She thought about it and said, "Maybe an average of $25 a week, so that's $1250 a year."

I said, "Would it be worth $1250 a year if once a week, particularly during hectic work weeks, you had dinner delivered instead of making it yourself? Would that free up some of your time? Would you enjoy it? Are you worth it?" She agreed on all counts. It's food for thought.

Be Kind to Yourself

The graduate student I spoke with had a hectic schedule. Besides taking several courses, she worked in the afternoons and was a volunteer for a service organization two nights a week. Some mornings, she barely made the bus. This kind of pressure had become routine, yet it was no way to start her day.

I listened closely to her story and asked, "How much is the bus ride to school?" She said it was $1.75. I said, "How much would a taxi ride cost?" She was aghast. "I couldn't take a taxi!" I said, "Wait a second. How much would a taxi ride be?" She didn't know, so we paused in our conversation. She called the closest taxi company and asked about the charges from her apartment to her class in the morning. At that time, the cost was about $6.50.

When she called me back, I popped the question: "How upsetting would it be to your budget if occasionally, when you're running late, you hail a taxi and pay $6.50 instead of paying $1.75 for the bus?" She said, "I suppose it wouldn't hurt."

I said, "You're right. You could hail a taxi as often as once a week, and in the course of a fifteen-week semester you're only paying an extra $97.50 for the luxury of not being enslaved to the bus schedule. We blow at least $97.50 on stuff all the time. Why not be gentle with yourself? Acknowledge that you're handling a lot in life right now, and occasionally you deserve to take a taxi ride to school." She relented.

Reflect and Win

How often do you become stuck in a miserly mode, pinching pennies here and there, while blowing triple or quadruple digits on items of marginal value?

If you're a big-city career-type, the same principle applies. If you're up on East 76th Street in Manhattan and have to make it to 44th in a hurry, once every week or so, it won't put a notable dent in your wallet to take a taxi rather than the subway or bus.

Great Time/Money Trades

What time/money trade-offs might make good sense in your situation? Many supermarkets and grocery markets will deliver for a nominal fee. Some offer hard copy or online catalogs from which you can order by phone, fax, e-mail, or website. For routine items, you can establish a standing order whereby every week the market delivers eggs, milk, whatever. You can still shop for new or specialty food items now and then, lugging all those bags home so you remember what it's like. It will reinforce your inclination to use grocery delivery services.

If you're buying presents and a store offers a wrapping service, pay the extra dollar and have them wrap it. Do you particularly want to fiddle with wrapping paper, tape, scissors, string, bows, and all that stuff? If you do, fine, that's your option. For another dollar (or whatever it takes), isn't it worth it to have that chore completed?

There even are people who can go shopping for you to buy gifts, shoes, or nearly anything. If you dislike shopping (or aren't too good at it) and someone you trust is good at it, this could make sense. The professional shopper can actually save you money. He or she knows where to find the best buys.

Maid for You: A Panoply of Service Providers

Hiring a maid can be beneficial, especially if you're an entrepreneur seeking local service providers. One cleaning service I retained, for example, offered a unique approach to speedy office and house cleaning. It would send six or eight people at once and finish the job within 45 minutes!

Here are other types of services that probably exist in your community (they'll be called something else in your city, of course).

➤ Gutters-R-Us (clears your gutters, saves you from roof duty)
➤ Jumpin' Jack Flash (pick-up and delivery)
➤ The Butler Did It (a catering service)
➤ Everything But Windows (housecleaning)
➤ Rent a Dad (house repair for the terminally unhandy)
➤ The Tree Doctor (tree- and hedge-trimming)
➤ Walkin' the Dog (cares for Pooch when you're gone—or when you're not)
➤ Shake a Leg (airport shuttle service)

All kinds of part-time workers are ready to help you as well, some more suitable to your needs than others. These include part-time regular employees, retirees, temporaries, and students: high school, college, intern, foreign-exchange, and grad school.

You probably can find a bright, motivated student to help you. Schools are full of intelligent, perceptive young men and women, many seeking an opportunity to gain some real-world experience. Their part-time status doesn't mean they're less intelligent or effective. Many can take a "divisible" unit of work and do a bang-up job on it.

What could helpers do for you? Take a look.

Reflect and Win

Most communities have high-school juniors and seniors who'd be thrilled to work for $.50 an hour above minimum wage. This might not seem like a lot of money to you, but it is to them.

What Helpers Could Do for You
➤   Serve routine customer needs.
➤   Make deliveries and pick-ups.
➤   Route/sort the mail.
➤   Answer requests for information.
➤   Send out mailings of any sort.
➤   Make first-round or lead calls to prospective customers.
➤   Hunt for a product or service you need.
➤   Catalog new information or products.
➤   Proofread or double-check anything written.
➤   Survey customers and their needs.
➤   Keep track of necessary data and news sources.
➤   Type mailing lists.
➤   Type anything, for that matter.
➤   Keep things tidy, clean, and in good repair.
➤   Study competitors, their literature, and their products.
➤   Track inventory or arrange displays.
➤   Do anything that a less-essential, part-time employee could do without excessive guidance.

Your new found mission: identify all those non-essential-but-bothersome tasks you've been putting off that a part-timer can handle.

The Time Master Says

Every time you successfully use one of your many helpers, you're preserving your time!

"Seed work" functions best when it's a distinct unit of work—easily assigned to someone else. For example, suppose you want information on the eight other local companies in your field. A high-school student can easily visit the web, open the phone book or a local trade publication, and summarize the information gathered. An experienced employee could then spot trends or innovations from this data, all with a minimum of your time spent on instruction.

Coming to Terms
Seed work is the sort of task you can easily assign to someone else because the downside risk if they botch the task is negligible.

Easy Steps to Developing Your Own Service System

Whether you live in a community of 38,000 or 1,038,000, many service providers can help you with domestic as well as business tasks to free you for whatever makes the most money for you.

Perhaps you now are enthusiastic about the prospects of bringing such providers into your life. If you start using such helpers in a systematic way, you'll be on the road to winning back your time.

Here are suggestions for putting your service system in place:

1. Identify all the tasks you don't like to do. Make this list as long as possible. Be honest with yourself. Separate the list into domestic and career-related tasks.
2. On two separate pages (one for domestic and one for career-related tasks) create a matrix listing these tasks down the left-hand side of each page. Across the top of each page, make three columns; label them Option 1 through Option 3:

	Option 1	Option 2	Option 3
Task A			
Task B			
Task C			
Task D			
Task E			

3. If you list five tasks down the left-hand side of the page for your domestic sheet, with three option boxes across the top of the page, potentially you have 15 cells to fill. Fill even half of them and you'll be in great shape.

4. Within the blank cells, list every alternative you can imagine for not doing tasks you don't enjoy doing. You might find yourself writing down such options as delegating the tasks to your kids, your neighbors' kids, or someone you found in a shopper's guide or the Yellow Pages.

5. Review your grid. If you don't have good options for some of the tasks, speak to your local librarian. Talk to the job placement officer at your local high school, community college, or university. Ask around. You're likely to get many names of people who can help you.

6. Interview, interview, interview. Over the phone is fine; in person is better. Map out what you want done; break in your helpers gently, but systematically.

7. Start a file of the literature or information you've collected on all the types of helpers you've been encountering. Once you have a file of helpers, keep adding to it, keep it current, and use it.

By following this seven part plan, you have only your time and life to win back!

CHAPTER 10

Becoming a Snooze-Savvy Sleeper

In This Chapter:

➤ You're probably not getting enough sleep
➤ Can you really catch up on your sleep?
➤ How too little sleep hinders your effectiveness
➤ How to enjoy more rest throughout the day

This chapter asks *are you getting enough sleep*? If not, why not? Because proper sleep dramatically impacts your effectiveness at work.

Study after study shows that most American adults have been depriving themselves of needed sleep. Dr. William Dement, founder of Stanford University's Sleep Center, observed that "most Americans no longer know what it feels like to be fully alert."

The Brain Keeps Track of Your Sleep Deficit

In his landmark book *The Promise of Sleep*, Dr. William Dement unequivocally states, "like bricks in a back pack, accumulated sleep drive is a burden that weighs you down. Every hour that you are awake adds another brick to the pack."

"The brain keeps an exact accounting of how much sleep it is owed," Dr. Dement notes. "Each successive night of partial loss is carried over and the end effect appears to accumulate in a precisely additive fashion . . . The size of the sleep debt and its dangerous effect are directly related to the amount of lost sleep . . ."

"In just a few decades of technological innovation we have managed to totally overthrow our magnificently evolved biological clocks, and the complex biorhythms they regulate."

How crucial is sleep in your quest to win back your time? How vital is it to your overall health and effectiveness? Highly important.

Sleep Deprivation: A Disaster in the Making

Short-changing your sleep on any *one* night won't cause you much harm. You might feel crummy the next day, but you can compensate by napping or retiring early the next evening.

In *The 24-Hour Society*, sleep-researcher Dr. Martin Moore-Ede found that getting less sleep than you need, day after day, can lead to disaster. Moore-Ede pinpoints a rash of plane, train, and other transportation mishaps that resulted due to insufficient sleep on the part of those in question.

How much do you need to sleep each day? It all depends—for some people, seven hours a night is great; for others, it's eight; for others, nine. Most adults need about eight hours. College students might need nine to nine-and-a-half hours (whether or not they stayed up until three in the morning, they still need more sleep than a 35-year-old). As people age, some need more than eight hours a night; some need less.

Jack D. Edinger, Ph.D., a leading insomnia researcher, says, "The older one gets, the less smooth one's sleep pattern. It is normal for someone between 40 and 70 to be awake some part of the night." As you age, you might need more than eight hours of sleep nightly if it's punctuated by wakeful periods (not uncommon).

You've long known that you need sufficient sleep to function effectively. Who, or what, is the culprit? Here are the suspects.

Bad Sleep Habits Hang Heavy

If you've gone to bed at 11:00 or midnight for the past several months, chances are you'll go to bed around the same time this evening. If you turn in only after some late night talk show host does his/her monologue, you've developed a habit of retiring late.

Alternatively, if you have all manner of things to read and hear surrounding you, it's tempting to stay up yet another 20 or 30 minutes—which can balloon into 40 to 60 minutes.

Many people remain awake longer when surrounded by information stimulants.

If you use drugs, especially alcohol, your sleep patterns will be disrupted. You're likely to end up with too little sleep. Alcohol might knock you out fast, but it can cause sleep difficulty and frequent wake-ups.

Coming to Terms

Midnight originally meant halfway through the night because people went to sleep when it got dark and got up when it became light.

The Maddening Phenomena of Microsleep

Your eyes might be open, but don't let that fool you. Moore-Ede found that many people engage in microsleep (the body's attempt to compensate for under-sleeping) throughout the day. For example, microsleep can occur when:

➤ bus drivers have full passenger loads.
➤ truck drivers are racing down hills hauling nuclear weapons.
➤ mothers are transporting their babies.

Coming to Terms

Microsleep is a 5-to-10-second episode when your brain is effectively asleep while you are otherwise up and about. Microsleep can occur while you are working at a PC or driving your car.

Drowsiness comes in waves. You can be alert one moment, drowsy the next, and not know the difference. Having too little sleep the night before (and certainly on an extended basis) increases the probability you'll engage in microsleep.

Rapid Eye Movements Every Night

Rapid eye movements, known as REM sleep, are a crucial part of your overall sleep cycle. If you sleep too little or are suddenly awakened, your REM pattern can be disrupted. Hence, even eight hours in bed might not yield the benefits of a solid eight-hour sleep.

Coming to Terms
Your eyes actually make rapid eye movements (REM) while your eyelids are closed; these correspond to various levels of brain activity that are essential to sound sleep.

To win back your waking time, protect your sleep time:

➤ Don't sleep with your head by a phone that can ring aloud. Remove the phone from your bedroom. Some people sleep with their heads by the phone because, say, they have aged loved ones far away. They worry about that one call in 15 years that might haul them out of bed at 3:00 a.m. There's not much anyone can do at that hour. You'd be better off having 15 years of sound sleep.

➤ Once a week, retire by 9:00 p.m. Your body will thank you. Let yourself go to dreamland for 9, 10, 11 hours—whatever it takes. You're probably going to live longer than you think you will; to reach old age with grace and ease, allow yourself at least one weeknight when sleep is your only objective.

➤ One Friday night each month, crash right after work and don't arise until the next morning to experience a fabulous Saturday morning. Have dinner or skip it, as suits you.

➤ Avoid caffeine for the six hours before retiring. This means if you retire at 10:00, 4:00 in the afternoon (or before) is the last time to imbibe any caffeine.

➤ Avoid alcohol in the evening. Sure, you'll fall asleep quickly, but then you'll awake too early, have trouble getting back to sleep, find that your overall sleep time is reduced, and incur poor quality sleep.

➤ If you fall asleep when you read in bed, fine, but don't overdo this. Dr. Edinger says it's important to make your bed and bedroom for sleeping (and, of course, sex) only. Don't set up your bed as a command station with gadgets and appliances that reinforce alertness.

➤ Retire when you're tired. Let your body talk. It'll tell you when it's tired. Have you ignored the message?

➤ Don't fret if you don't fall asleep right away. You might need some time. After 30 consecutive minutes of restlessness, do something else until you're tired again.

➤ Moderate exercise several hours before sleep aids in getting sound sleep.

➤ Moderate intake of proteins, such as a glass of milk, also aids in sound sleep.

Catching Up on Sleep: Myth or Reality?!

If you've been depriving yourself of sleep for the last three years, you can't literally add back all the hours you missed.

Nevertheless, your body is extremely forgiving. Ex-cigarette smokers know this. Lungs abused by years of smoking, if permanent damage has not commenced, begin to cleanse themselves once the smoking stops for good. The effects of ten years of abuse can greatly diminish in as little as one year. So it is with chronic under-sleeping.

Getting enough sleep, as with engaging in other healthy practices, is a habit. Albert Gray, an entrepreneur of yesteryear, said, "Every single qualification of success is acquired through habit. Men (and women) form habits, and habits form futures. If you do not deliberately form good habits, then unconsciously you will form bad ones."

Pause!
Dr. Martin Moore-Ede notes that if you stay up too late one evening, you are borrowing from the next day.

The Time Master Says
Even if you've deprived yourself of sleep for a prolonged period, if you devote the next month to giving yourself all the sleep you that can, you'll be in reasonably fine shape.

Depriving yourself of sleep is a bad habit. Of course you have a lot to do. You'll complete it all more effectively with sufficient sleep, not with less sleep.

Here are several suggestions to develop (or perhaps redevelop) the habit of getting sufficient sleep:

➤ Let others know about your newfound quest—this means family members who might otherwise impede your progress.
➤ One weekend day (or more) per month, linger longer in the morning before rising— you know, sleep in!
➤ Any time you're traveling for work, give the TV remote control to the front desk at the hotel. You can't afford to be still clicking away at midnight. Get sleep when you're on the road (more on this shortly).
➤ Schedule extra sleep any time you're on vacation. An extra 30–45 minutes can make all the difference in the quality of your vacation.
➤ Recognize that at first you might have to force yourself to get into bed, even if it is 9:00 or 9:30 on a weekday evening and you'd rather be up and around.

How Do You Know if You're Sleep Deficient?

Only you can determine how much sleep you need. Start at square one: review this list of items that indicate you're probably not having enough sleep. Some of these might be familiar, some might be news to you:

➤ You bump into things more often than is normal for you.
➤ You slur your words.
➤ You have trouble digesting food.
➤ You're short with people when normally you wouldn't be.
➤ Your eyes are tired.
➤ Your joie de vivre is missing.
➤ You don't enjoy sex as much as you used to.
➤ You need to wake up by alarm clock (many people don't need an alarm, they arise on their own).
➤ You don't want to face the day.
➤ Even small tasks seem to loom larger.
➤ Your life has achieved a level of fine monotony.
➤ You find it easier to engage in tasks that don't involve talking to others.
➤ As much as you hate going to the dentist, you find leaning back in the dentist's chair rather relaxing.
➤ You find yourself nodding off in what are otherwise interesting and/or important meetings.
➤ You zone out for unknown periods of time while working.

If you're deficient by more than ten hours a week, as a benchmark, it'll take you about a month to "recover." Recovery doesn't mean you can replace all the hours you've lost. It means that you can arrive at the point where you're fully functional and minimize (or perhaps eradicate) the effects of past deprivation.

I know I've had all the sleep I need when I'm ready to bolt out of bed in the morning, ready to start the day. To determine your optimal sleep time, consider the following:

➤ Experiment with the number of hours you sleep each night, for one week. Start with eight hours, say 10:30 p.m. to 6:30 a.m.
➤ If eight hours feels good, stay right there; no need to move on. If not, increase the amount by 15-minute increments.
➤ If you awake before you've slept eight hours (and you do not nap excessively during the day), perhaps you need less than eight hours.
➤ To make your test valid, give up your alarm clock! Yes, give it up (any time you can afford to—not, of course, when you have a plane to catch). When you awake by alarm, you don't know how long you would have slept.

Daytime Snooze Rules

If you have the chance, taking naps throughout the day (even weekdays) can enhance your overall effectiveness and put you in the driver's seat of winning back your time.

Some people nap without problems; others can't nap at all. One study found that if you nap for 30 minutes each afternoon, you actually have a 30 percent lower incidence of heart disease than people who don't nap at all. Napping increases your alertness for the rest of the day. Although many people feel a bit groggy for a few minutes after a nap, it gradually subsides and they feel more alert (and in a better mood).

The Time Master Says
The extra edge napping provides can last for eight to ten hours. However, naps are not designed to be substitutes for missed nocturnal sleep.

Short naps are actually more productive than long naps. A short nap will leave you refreshed, whereas a long nap might interfere with your sleep that evening. The best nap time is between 2:00 p.m. and 3:00 p.m. Any later, and your nap might be too deep, interfering with your nightly sleep.

If you can, nap in a bed or a cot, but not a chair. Your quality of sleep will be higher and the immediate benefits more apparent; however, naps aren't a substitute for the proper amount of sleep.

Sleepy or Dehydrated?

Hydration and dehydration play an important role in how much sleep you need.

About half the time I feel tired during the day it is because I haven't taken in enough water. Nutritionist David Meinz of Orlando, Florida, says every chemical reaction in your body requires water. In fact, your brain is 75 percent water.

Coming to Terms
When you're hydrated, your body's tissues are sufficiently filled with water. To be dehydrated is to be parched.

Meinz says that your thirst mechanisms lag behind your true need for water on a continual basis. Even a two percent reduction in your amount of body water will render you less productive than normal. A five percent reduction can seriously decrease mental functioning. Here are Meinz's suggestions for ensuring you're sufficiently hydrated:

➤   Eight cups of water a day is the standard, but don't wait until your thirst reminds you that you need water. Drink before you're thirsty.

➤   If you exercise a lot, your body requires a full 24 hours to regain the water supply that you need. Hence, you have to have much more water than you think when you work out.

➤   Drink eight ounces of water before starting your workout. During your workout, drink as often as you can.

➤   Register with the best water-delivery service in your area, or buy bottled water. The best choices for bottled water are distilled water or spring water.

➤   If you use tap water, let it run about 30 seconds so any sediments can run off.

Meinz also says to take a multivitamin every day to reduce feelings of lethargy and ensure that you're getting most of the basic nutrients. Along with sufficient water intake, this will help you feel more vibrant more often during your day.

Getting Rest Throughout the Day

Here are other ways to rest throughout the day without diminishing your overall output:

➤   Find a quiet place in your office, such as an empty conference room or a coworker's office, where you can sit in a chair for a few minutes and be still without fear of interruption. Even two minutes can help recharge your batteries.

➤   Go outside to a bench, your car, or other safe haven where you can do the same.

➤   Linger for an extra minute or two after eating your lunch; this helps you to better digest your food.

➤   Rest while you walk. This sounds like a contradiction, but you can walk hurriedly or stroll restfully. On your way back from the restroom, a coworker's office, or lunch, stroll mindfully down the hall in a rhythmic fashion, fast enough that no one will accuse you of being a zombie, but sufficiently slow that you're hardly exerting yourself. This technique can work wonders.

➤   Practice the same restful habits outlined above, on Saturday and Sunday, as well as during the week. Who says you have to go all out during the weekend? Obviously, the opportunities for outright naps are greater on Saturday and Sunday, so take them.

What about when you're feeling drowsy but you have to be awake and alert? In that case, think light and cool. With bright lights, your sense of alertness is enhanced and your brain is switched on. In essence, brightness equals wakefulness.

If your work area is somewhat chilly (say, 68 degrees or less), you're likely to stay more attentive and alert. When making presentations, it's better to have an audience cool and awake than warm and sleepy.

Getting Good Sleep on the Road

Suppose you're bedding down for the night in a hotel and need a good night's sleep so that you can summon enough energy to hold your own at the meeting the next day. Unluckily, the guest from hell is in the next room and at 2:30 a.m. apparently is trying to break the decibel barrier. You're a sound sleeper, but this night you're tossing and turning for hours before dozing off.

What can you do after checking into your hotel room to ensure that you achieve a good night's sleep, every night, regardless of the quality of your sleeping accommodations?

Suppose noise is invading the room you've rented. If it's easy enough to determine the direction of the sound, and if the intrusion is from the room to the left or right, you could try tapping (gently but firmly) on the wall. This alone sometimes works. In many hotels, the phone system allows you to readily dial adjacent rooms. If the noise is from across the hall or above or below you, call the night manager to handle the situation.

Employing Sleep Tools

At home, or away, to maintain greater control of potential sound disturbances, some essential items you can use before checking into any hotel room include: a "sound screen," earplugs, and a timer.

➤ The *Sound Screen* is a portable white-noise device developed by the Marpac Corporation, www.marpac.com. The *Sound Screen* emits different frequencies and amplitudes of a droning, non-disruptive blanket of sound. You can use this device to minimize the effects of startling or disruptive sounds outside your

Coming to Terms
A sound screen creates a sound "barrier" that breaks up, masks, or mutes the effects of louder sound from beyond the barrier by using white noise (a sound much like that of rushing water).

room. By placing the screen about ten feet from your head in the direction of any disruptive noise, you minimize the intrusive effects immediately.

➤ Create your own white noise. If you're awakened and the offending noise isn't too outrageous, use an empty channel on your TV set or radio as a white-noise machine. If you're using a TV this way, turn the brightness down to nothing, or cover the screen set with a blanket or towel to minimize light from the screen. If the TV isn't bolted down, put it between you and the noise. Experiment with your room's thermostat. Perhaps you can turn on the fan.

➤ Earplugs are available at many drug stores. They cost little and weigh even less. Airline gate and runway crews use ear plugs to shut out heavy-duty noise. The plugs expand in your outer ear canal, blocking sound in ways traditional earplugs cannot.

➤ An essential device is your own alarm clock or cell phone timer. You can wake up on cue and be free from having to keep your room phone plugged in. When you remove the plug from the phone, be sure to position the cord so the end is exposed to you; it will remind you to plug it back in when you awaken.

Remaining Well-Rested and Ready

If you're committed to experiencing the level of sleep and rest you need, and if you're looking forward to being more alert and refreshed during the workday, you're well on the way to making this happen. While you'll feel the difference, nevertheless here's a checklist of indicators that let you know you're getting the amount of sleep you need.

➤ You look forward to facing the day.

➤ You no longer need an alarm clock to awake.

➤ You awaken with energy, feeling great.

➤ Your eyes look clear, not red and bloodshot.

➤ You put in a full workday

➤ You have deep satisfaction about what you accomplish.

➤ You have sufficient energy for activities after work.

➤ You look forward to sex.

➤ Your joie de vivre is back.

Pause!

Although sleep needs vary, people who sleep about eight hours, on average, tend to live longer. "There will always be people who think that they can handle the affects of fatigue or believe that they can train themselves to slip by with less sleep to get more work done," sleep pioneer William Dement, Ph.D. observed. "All scientific evidence available says that this isn't so."

PART 3

Taking Back
Your Turf

Part 3
Taking Back Your Turf

Does it feel sometimes as if you're being boxed in on all sides at work? You've likely incurred some encroachment of your time, space, and room to maneuver.

If you can reduce requests for your time, you'll be able to tackle your office and desk. A desk is not a filing cabinet; window sills and the corners of your room are not permanent storage locations. Then you can manage piles and trials with smiles, and investigate some low-cost technology that won't drain your brain to use.

When you make it to that point, we can move on to clever ways to handle all the messages that have been bombarding you.

CHAPTER 11

Loan Yourself Out Less and Be Happier

In This Chapter:

➤ What to do when your boss wants you to be a workaholic
➤ Defend your calendar, because it's your life
➤ Learning to say no with grace and ease
➤ How to get off—and stay off—mailing lists

In this chapter you'll discover the importance of being more judicious with your calendar, because tomorrow's promises that you make to others arrive sooner than you think.

Actor Robert Redford once said, "Washington is a receptacle for workaholics." He could have said that about New York, Chicago, or many other major metro areas. The array of available technology provides you the opportunity to do far more in a day than your predecessors of yesteryear. Concurrently, it gives your boss and your organization the opportunity to expect more from you. Once you could generate a handful of letters each day, with luck. Now, with mere keystrokes, you can crank out 1,000 messages and still have time to work yourself to exhaustion before the day's end.

The More You Accomplish, the More Expected of You

In today's work environment, the more you can do, the more that is expected of you. Unfortunately, expectations about what you can accomplish rise immediately with the introduction of tools that facilitate greater accomplishment. This explains why you frequently feel squashed in the gears of your work life, like a present-day version of Charlie Chaplin in *Modern Times*. Instead of working on a real assembly line with which you cannot keep pace, your "assembly line" is digital, byte-sized, and cyber-driven at nearly the speed of light.

Pause!
You're a good worker and happy to help your organization in meaningful ways. Unfortunately, not all organizations make reasonable demands, especially if business has been slow lately.

Survivors of Downsizing

The Family's and Work Institute conducted a survey years back of workers who remained after downsizing efforts by their respective organizations and found that

➤ 59% lacked time for reflection,
➤ 56% couldn't complete their assigned tasks,
➤ 55% felt overwhelmed by the work load,
➤ 54% felt overworked, and
➤ 45% felt compelled to multitask too often.

Those who remain after a downsizing face a tough road fraught with time pressures and anxieties. Yet, in organizations where downsizing has not occurred, or at least not recently occurred, many of the same feelings among staff predominate!

Uneven and Unfair for Remaining Workers

If a department is caught shorthanded, or if someone retires, makes a career change, or simply departs for whatever reason, the workload falls to those who remain. In companies of all sizes, or within tightly run departments, the absence of employees temporarily results in an uneven workload for those present.

Whether your organization has experienced a down turn or you simply

The Time Master Says
In 2001, when General Colin Powell became Secretary of State, he gave a closed door, stirring speech about the mission of the agency and his personal vision. He also discussed the importance of going home at a reasonable hour, not working on weekends, and maintaining a sense of balance.

are asked to do too much too often, you need to take charge of your turf and win back your time. Let's start with the vital challenge of managing your boss.

Teach Your Boss to Treat You Right

Whole books have been written on this subject! In a single sentence: ultimately, you'll be treated by your boss in the way you teach your boss to treat you.

Look around your organization. Who is stepped on the most? Who is handled with kid gloves? Generally, the office wimps are treated as doormats, and those a bit more finicky are treated with a tad more respect. The key to not having your boss consume the time in your life beyond the normal workday involves re-examining the issues discussed in Chapter 1, "The Overtime Epidemic: How to Nip It in the Bud," and learning specific phrases that you can offer as needed. Read on.

Pause!
You don't want to be an office wimp, an unsung hero who's directed to perform feats of productivity simply because you can, with no regard to your personal well-being.

When Your Boss is a Workaholic

Suppose your boss is a workaholic and expects you to be the same. This situation requires tact and professionalism because you can't change your boss's nature. You are likely to be confronted with his or her workaholism and its effect on you. Here are key phrases that might help (and they work even better if your boss is not a workaholic!) Commit these to memory; often it's vital that your retort be automatic.

➤   "I'm over-committed right now, and if I take that on I can't do it justice."
➤   "I appreciate your confidence in me. I wouldn't want to take this on knowing my other tasks and responsibilities right now would prohibit me from doing an excellent job."
➤   "I'd be happy to handle this assignment for you, but realistically I can't do it without foregoing some other things I'm working on. Of tasks A and B, which would you like me to do? Which can I put aside?"

➤ "I can do that for you. Will it be okay if I respond to you next Wednesday? I currently have a, b, and c in the queue."

➤ "The number of tasks and complexity of assignments I'm handling is mounting. Perhaps we could look at a two- or four-week scenario of what's most important to you, such as when the assignments need to be completed and what I can realistically handle over that time period."

Even workaholic bosses are appreciative of your efforts on occasion. When the boss knows that you naturally work hard, he or she is not as likely to impose on you so often. A great time to make a sterling effort is when the boss is away. Most people follow the old adage, "When the cat's away, the mice will play."

After the boss has returned, be the one who is able say, "Here's that big report you wanted. It's all done."

When the boss is traveling or simply downtown on appointments, that's when he or she is most likely to monitor who's doing what back at the office. That's when the boss calls into the office more frequently, inspects things more closely upon returning, and is more on-edge, knowing that many employees have slacked off. So, this is your chance to shine, to teach this workaholic that you don't need to be over-monitored, and to make great strides toward controlling your time.

Reflect and Win

If you're the one who works hard when the boss is away, you help to convey a message that he or she doesn't need to constantly keep heaping on assignments.

Calendar on the Wall, Who's Over Committed Most of All?

When you look at your calendar months in advance and there's nothing scheduled, that's when you fall into time-traps. Suppose Jim comes in and asks you to volunteer for a charitable cause he supports. It's not until three months from today. You look at your schedule and see that the time is open. So you say, "Sure, why not?" You schedule the event accordingly, and you intend to honor your commitment.

Two months pass. As you approach the date on which you promised Jim you'd volunteer, you notice that you have responsibilities in and around it. A day or two before the time you're scheduled to help Jim, your schedule is jam-packed. Suddenly, Jim's long-standing request looks like an intrusion. Yet, when he asked and you agreed, it all seemed so harmless. All of which leads to Jeff's Law of Defending Your Calendar, which states:

An empty calendar is not such a bad thing.

Quiz question: why are you inclined to schedule tasks as a volunteer, but you aren't inclined to schedule leisure-time activities, particularly those on a weekday after work? Hopefully, you have no trouble scheduling a vacation. What about scheduling fun, relaxing and leisure activities? Defend your calendar on a continual basis!

On the heels of 500 other things you have to do, it might not be appropriate or even feasible for you to take on another task at this time.

Your life, as discussed in Chapter 1— as well as your career, year, month, workweek, and day—are finite. Your calendar, essentially, is your life— therefore, you need to defend it.

As an exercise, review old calendars and examine your appointments, activities, and tasks. How many things that you scheduled could you have done without?. In reviewing my own prior calendars (before I got all this wisdom), I found 50 percent of my activities were nonessential. Most could be cut because they weren't in accordance with my priorities and goals. I either yielded to the whim of the moment, or I hadn't developed the ability to say no.

Here's a quick list of techniques to help you determine whether you can safely avoid adding some future commitment to your calendar:

Reflect and Win

Volunteering to help others is a worthy endeavor. Services and contributions by volunteers propel society. Without volunteers, many social institutions would wither away.

Coming to Terms

A whim is a sudden or odd notion, often unexplained or unusual.

➤ Is it in alignment with your priorities and goals?
➤ Are you as likely to say yes to such a request next week?
➤ What else could you do at that time that would be more rewarding?
➤ What other pressing tasks are you likely to face around that time?
➤ Does the other party have options besides you? Is "no" fatal to them?
➤ Do you like the other party?

If none of the above work, make your decision in three days, particularly when you can respond by phone, mail, email, or text. It's easier to decline when you don't have to do so in person.

Pause!

If you don't defend your calendar, it will surely be filled in with all manner of seemingly *worthwhile* activities.

Learn to Say No Gracefully

The bigger your organization, the more requests you receive to attend or support various functions. If you're an entrepreneur, or even a student or a retiree, you still are likely to face many requests. With Edgar's retirement party, Megan's baby shower, Kevin's summer bash, Aunt Sarah's 64th birthday party, the Little League parade, and who knows what else, it would be easy for you to fill up your calendar and never finish your job—let alone do the things you want to do in life. Most requests can be handled aptly with a polite "no."

You don't need to bone up on the advice of Amy Vanderbilt or Miss Manners to say no with grace and ease. Employ any of the following responses as they apply:

➤ The easiest technique you can use to decline a request is to say that your child's birthday/recital/graduation will be occurring at that time, and you couldn't miss it. Undoubtedly, your child will be doing something that merits your presence!

➤ Cite anything your family has planned. For example, "Oh, that's the day our family is taking our annual fall foliage trip. We planned it months ago, and the hotel reservations have already been made. I do appreciate your asking."

➤ Say, "I'd like to, but I'm so overcommitted right now I couldn't work on it and do it justice."

➤ "I wish you had asked me a couple of days ago. I already committed that time to helping XYZ accomplish ABC."

➤ "Could I take a rain-check on that one? I've been working myself dizzy lately, and I've scheduled that time already."

If you have no legitimate prevailing circumstances, here are other possible responses:

➤ "Let me get back to you by tomorrow on that." Tomorrow, use the aforementioned phone, mail, email, or text messaging to politely decline.

➤ Offer a gently worded "Thanks, but I need to pass on that."

Simplification = Freedom

You face so much that competes for your time and attention—perhaps a workaholic boss, an overfilled calendar, or scads of future commitments. Don't volunteer to have others hit you with even more tasks. The next time somebody calls with a highly worthwhile information service that you can subscribe to, politely decline.

In addition, the following techniques for handling subscriptions might be of use to you:

> **Reflect and Win**
> Without thinking, do you add your name to mailing lists, openly surrendering yourself to more data and more offers? If you make yourself aware of which organizations or businesses sell their client or membership lists, you can avoid the mailing-list blues.

➤   As each of your subscriptions expire, don't immediately renew. Wait two months to see if you miss having the publication. If you don't, then you've saved some money and lots of time.

➤   If you do miss it, then re-subscribe. The vendor will take you back, and in many cases, you'll even receive a better rate.

➤   For the publications you currently receive, immediately strip them down; tear out or photocopy only those articles or passages that appear to be of interest to you. Then recycle the rest of the publication. (See the next chapters.)

➤   For existing subscriptions, experiment with giving away every second or third issue. Even chemists, engineers, and highly technical types agree they could skip every third issue of their technical publications and not be less informed; most periodicals have an inherent redundancy.

➤   Each year, many magazines publish a roster of all the articles that they featured in their final issue of the year. Such indices can be invaluable; you can highlight exactly which articles you would like to see.

➤   Many publications maintain an online version whereby you can acquire the specific articles you desire.

The Value of Eliminating Unwanted Mail

By extending the principles of reducing your magazine glut to your mail, you ultimately can save even more time. To get off—and stay off—mailing lists, write to the Mail Preference Service and ask to be removed from the list:

Mail Preference Service
Direct Marketing Association
P.O. Box 9008
Farmingdale, NY 11735–9008

➤ When you write, include all variations of your name, such as Jeff Davidson, Jeffrey P. Davidson, Jeffrey Davidson, J. Davidson, J. P. Davidson, and so on; do this for all others in your household for maximum effectiveness.

➤ Thereafter, write to the organization every four months with a follow-up reminder; any purchase you make by credit card or check is likely to return your name to the direct-mail rolls.

➤ Create a printed label that says:

"I don't want my name placed on any mailing lists whatsoever, and I forbid the use, sale, rental, or transfer of my name."

➤ When you are besieged by third-class mail from repeat or gross offenders, and when such offenders have included a self-addressed bulk-mail reply envelope, feel free to use the envelope to request that your name be removed from their lists. Also, re-view their literature to see if there is a (toll-free) 800-, 888-, or 877-, 866-, 855- or 844--number by which you can make such a request, at no cost to you.

➤ Inform the parties with whom you do business that you do not appreciate having your name added to a mailing list and being inundated by catalogs, eblasts, announcements, and fliers. This step is essential if you place an order online.

CHAPTER 12

The Efficiently-Organized Office

In This Chapter:

➤ Guarding the flat surfaces of your life
➤ Handling paper more quickly and easily
➤ What to chuck and what to retain
➤ Times not to Disturb You

This chapter helps you to tackle the major task of whipping your office into shape, which ultimately enhances your use of time.

On the road to taking charge of your turf, you've learned two key principles thus far. In Chapter 10, "Becoming A Snooze-Savvy Sleeper," you read about the dramatic impact sleep can have on the quality of your life and your effectiveness, both on and off the job. In Chapter 11, "Loaning Yourself Out Less and Being Happier Because of It," you saw some ways that you volunteer (perhaps unwittingly) to have more assignments, commitments, and information thrown your way—and that it's possible to keep much of this at bay.

Control Your Desk, or It Will Control You

Despite long-standing promises of a paperless society, clutter is rising at an alarming rate at home and in the office. Many people now have more than one inbox. Too many people neglect their offices and their desks. Your mission: keep your desk clear!

In the movie *Top Gun*, Tom Cruise plays a Navy fighter pilot. Among his many responsibilities is flying expensive Navy aircraft and landing jets safely on aircraft carrier decks.

A few months after seeing the movie, I read an article in *Smithsonian* magazine about how aircraft carrier decks have to be completely clean and clear before a plane can land.

"All hands on deck" on an aircraft carrier deck meant that everyone—even senior officers—picked up a push broom and swept the deck completely clear when a plane was due to land. Today, giant blowers and vacuums do the job. The goal is the same: to leave nothing on the surface of the deck, not even a paper clip. This ensures the highest probability of a successful landing for everyone involved.

What happens if there is debris on the deck as a plane approaches? What if an earlier plane has not left the landing strip? The approaching plane is likely to crash and burn.

The Time Master Says

Your desktop is like the deck of an aircraft carrier. If you take the next pile of stuff that accumulates and simply park it in the corner of your desk hoping an organizing fairy will drop by and do something with it, good luck!

No one is coming to help you manage your desk; each new item you pile on will (figuratively) crash and burn as your work accumulates, unless you take charge of the situation.

All other things being equal, if you have but one project, one piece of paper, whatever you're working on, in front of you and the rest of your desk is clear, you're bound to have more energy, focus, and direction. If all manner of distractions compete for your attention—piles of reports and documents—how can you have the same focus, energy, and direction on the task at hand?

Your Desktop Is Not a Filing Cabinet

What to keep on top of your desk is uniquely individual. Anything you use on a daily basis (such as a stapler, roll of tape, or pen), generally stays on top of your desk. Otherwise, remove anything you can safely eliminate from your desktop. Where does it go? You might have a credenza behind you. If you're

Reflect and Win

The fewer items you have in vital places, the greater the sense of control you have over your immediate environment. Clear out the unnecessary items and start enjoying a new, more efficient work life.

thinking, "You asked me merely to shift my stuff from one surface to another," you're right. And it works!

Inside your desk, retain items you use weekly, if not daily—but don't start storing supplies there. Those belong farther away from you, in file cabinets or supply lockers. Your goal is to maintain the optimal number of items on and in your desk—enough so you work efficiently every day, but not enough to clutter up the works.

Extend Your Efforts to the Rest of the Room

After you've cleared your desk of what's unnecessary, apply the same principle to the top of your filing cabinet, closet shelves, and other areas.

What about your dining room table, a work bench, or the trunk or glove compartment of your car? Your goal is to have, in front of you, the few items you need and not much more. Once your flat surfaces are under control, you gain a heightened sense of control over your time.

Reflect and Win
Manage your desktop as if it's one of the most important elements to winning back your time—because it is.

Be the First on Your Block to Master Your Shelves

Shelves are a great invention, right up there with fire and the wheel. What best belongs on a shelf versus what goes in a filing cabinet? Filing is the subject of Chapter 13, "Becoming a Filing Wizard," so let's focus on the first part of the question here; what goes on your shelves? In a nutshell, your shelves are the home of the following items:

➤ Items you're bound to use within the next two weeks
➤ Items too large for a filing cabinet (or collections of such items)
➤ Projects in progress
➤ Supplies that can't go in supply cabinets

Let's examine each of these individually.

For Use within the Next Two Weeks

These include reference books, directories, manuals, instruction guides, books, and magazines (especially large ones, like annual directories and theme issues.)

If It Doesn't Fit, Shelve It

Because it's difficult to file some thick items such as books (and some magazines) or oversized items in a filing cabinet, any such item is better housed on a shelf. Any item that won't fit in a file cabinet (and any item that is part of a series) is probably best housed on your shelves.

If you receive a key industry publication and it makes sense for you to hang on to back issues, these also belong on your shelves. In this case, you could acquire magazine holders—essentially precut or preassembled boxes (corrugated cardboard or plastic) that hold about 24 issues of a monthly magazine.

Projects in Progress

If you're working on a project that requires a variety of items, the magazine boxes work well. If you have shelves behind your desk seat, keep one shelf compartment clear so you can lay incoming file folders flat on it. It's better to have these materials behind you than right in your immediate work area. Also, it makes sense to have a single flat surface (even among your shelving units) readily available to accommodate active files.

Supplies in Supply Cabinets!

Many people have little difficulty filling up their shelves. While your inclination might be to acquire more shelves, it's best to avoid that. Your goal is to keep your office or work area in shape within reasonable parameters—using the desk, filing cabinet, shelves, or supply cabinet you already have. If any of these is always overfilled, perhaps you do need to acquire another, but more often, lack of space is an excuse for not being able to manage an office.

Treat your shelves as somewhat sacred; align them so you can pull out key items at will. If it takes you longer than 30 seconds to find something on your shelves, refine your system.

Keep supplies in a supply cabinet because you can store them in bulk. Stack them horizontally, vertically, or one type of item on top of another.

Filing Finesse in Regard to Your Shelves

Filing is a dynamic process. Items you place in a file folder today might find their way onto your shelves, re-emerge in some other form, or be chucked. What's on your shelves might (in some mutant form) find its way into your files. If you have a big reference book on a shelf, you might have to extract a few pages from it, discard or recycle the larger volume, and retain only a few essential pages in a folder in your filing cabinet.

The relationship among all your storage areas is dynamic; your prevailing quest is to boil down what's crucial for you to retain—keep only the essence.

Clearing Out the Unnecessary

Are you fearful about tossing something because you fret that you're going to need it tomorrow? No discernible negative consequences to tossing something means you can toss it. Most of what you're retaining is readily replaceable anyway. Office efficiency experts claim that we never use 80 percent of what we file. Even if that's only partially true, it still means a significant chunk of what you're retaining is deadwood.

Clearing the deadwood from your desk, files, and office keeps your work space in shape. That enhances your capacity to handle new demands. It also improves the odds that you'll be able to locate those items you actually need.

Reflect and Win

Information is power; if you can't find what you've retained, it's of no value to you. Worse, the time you took to read and file the items would then be wasted.

Pause!

You could employ stacking trays, but they tend to become semi-permanent collections of paper rather than projects in progress.

Consider the cumulative time savings you could chalk up if you cut your search time in half. If you save only 12 minutes per day, that adds up to an hour per week and 50 hours per year. That's like creating an extra week for your self. Meanwhile, others in your office see that you're someone who is able to remain in control, find things quickly, and stay on top of situations. So, keeping your files (and office) in shape yields a multiple payoff.

The Time Master Says

Keeping things organized takes time, but persevere. The small time investment you make in developing your newfound efficiency will pay off repeatedly down the road.

Surround Yourself to Win Through Ergonomics

Ergonomics is the science of fitting the job to the worker. The office equipment you use, and how so, has an impact on your health, well-being, productivity, and your use of time. Healthy workers make more efficient workers. When the physical requirements of a job don't match the physical capacity of the workers, musculoskeletal disorders can result.

Keep Yourself and Others Injury Free

An ergonomic office helps prevent injuries due to cumulative trauma from repetitive tasks, such as typing. If you work in an organization that promotes wellness, see if you can have your seat, desk, and computer monitor aligned so that they are at the proper height and the correct settings for you.

Coming to Terms
Ergonomics is the science that examines how devices most smoothly blend with the human body and human activity.

If you're having back problems because of your chair, your wrists hurt, or something else is askew, you are not going to be at your productive best. You might end up taking sick days that you otherwise could avoid. Not getting a good night's sleep every night compounds the problem.

Pause!
The costs of cumulative trauma injuries can be considerable. Avoidable afflictions such as carpal tunnel syndrome and back strain cut into workers' productivity, sometimes forcing people to miss work or even change careers altogether. Experts estimate that the hidden costs of cumulative trauma injuries (lost productivity, absenteeism, and turnover) are *2 to 7 times* greater than the visible costs!

Pre-empt the Potential for Pain

If you manage others, before your staff complains of sore forearms, aching wrists, or lower back pain, invest in making your office ergonomic. Showing concern for their well-being also helps build loyalty, boost morale, and improve retention. If that's insufficient incentive, consider data from the U.S. Occupational Safety and Health Administration:

➤ Work-related musculoskeletal disorders account for 34% of all workday illnesses and injuries.

➤ More than 2,000,000 workers experience repetitive stress injuries each year.

➤ Workman's compensation claims due to physical stress have more than tripled since 1980. Most claims are relate to poor ergonomic conditions.

➤ About half of every dollar spent on medical costs will be for treating cumulative trauma disorders.

➤ Indirect costs (overtime, replacement, attorney fees) from work-related musculoskeletal disorders to U.S. businesses costs tens of billions per year.

Prevention through Ergonomics Pays

One study sponsored by State Farm Insurance found that clerical workers' performance improved by 15% with ergonomically suitable workstations and seating. Buying ergonomic furniture or other equipment and hiring consultants to teach your workers how to protect themselves against injuries can be expensive. However, the costs incurred by not making those investments are much higher.

Resources for becoming ergonomically correct abound:

Health and Wellness-related Websites

www.heart.org American Heart Association site
www.apa.org American Psychological Association site
www.jazzercise.com Dance Exercise sites
www.ergonomicresource.com Ergonomic Resource
www.ergonomicsmadeeasy.com Ergonomics Made Easy
www.ergoweb.com ErgoWeb, Inc.
www.office-ergo.com Office Ergo
www.officeworld.com Office World
www.sleepnet.com/depriv.htm Sleep Deprivation links
www.sourceequipment.com Source Equipment Company, Inc.
www.workspaces.com Work Spaces

Massage and Bodywork Sites

www.naturopathic.org
www.polaritytherapy.or
www.amtamassage.org American Massage Therapy Association

If your office ergonomics seem lacking, here are five steps to improve them:

1. *Set up computer stations properly.* Desks usually are designed for writing, not for computing.
2. *Buy adjustable chairs.* Ensure your chairs have adjustable heights, rotating five-wheel bases, tilting seats, and adjustable back rests.
3. *Keep muscles loose by providing support and adjusting position.* Proper support for sensitive body parts encourages blood flow, which carries oxygen to muscles and carts away waste.
4. *Set up desks so that workers can avoid repeating difficult tasks.* For example, a worker shouldn't have to make an awkward reach for a frequently used folder.
5. *If someone experiences physical discomfort at work, act at once.* A small delay can turn a small problem into a major one.

A Workout for the Cyber Set

For knowledge workers and career professionals iwho generally sit at a desk for much of the day, in addition to the ergonomic tips above, here are measures for overcoming sedentary inclinations that can quickly arise:

➤ Breathe in slowly through your nose, hold it for two seconds, and then exhale through your mouth. Repeat this several times, and you'll likely experience an energy boost.

➤ Roll your shoulders forward five or six times using a wide circular motion; do the same thing, this time rolling in the opposite direction.

➤ Turn your head slowly from side to side and look over each shoulder. Count to three. Repeat the exercise five to ten times.

➤ While in your chair, slowly bend your upper body between your knees. Stay this way for a few seconds, then sit up and relax. Repeat this once or twice to stretch your back.

➤ Hold your arms straight out in front of you. Raise and lower your hands, bending them at your wrists. Repeat this several times; it stretches the muscles in your forearms and gives your wrists relief.

➤ Fold your arms in front of you, raise your elbows to shoulder level, and then push them straight back. Hold this for a couple of seconds. This gives your upper back and shoulder blades some relief. Repeat five to ten times.

Take a break now and then. Ultimately, you'll accomplish more. And if you do even a few of these exercises, you'll feel better about your time during the workday and afterward.

Home Offices Require Quiet

Do you work at home? Many first-time home-based workers are in for a huge surprise—disturbances in and around the home can be as disconcerting as a traditional office! You need to establish physical, psychological, and auditory boundaries.

For example, when do you not wish to be disturbed? Perhaps you need to post the times. Establish a routine so that you work the same hours every day and everyone in your household knows it.

Reflect and Win

Many home-based workers find that their highest productivity comes early in the day, perhaps before everyone else wakes and often after everyone else departs.

CHAPTER 13

Becoming a Filing Wizard

In This Chapter:

➤ As the world grows more complex, filing becomes more important
➤ The essential tools for mastering the high art of filing
➤ It's both what you file and how you file it
➤ Design your filing system to uniquely serve the way you work

---

This chapter asks *do you look upon filing as drudgery?* If so, you're not alone! Since paper will be with us for at least a few more years, here we will formally tackle the issue.

You don't see people shooting movies, writing Broadway plays, or producing hard rock albums on the topic. It's rather mundane, even pedestrian. Yet it's an unheralded activity to winning back your time.

As we've discussed, when you're in control of your desk, office, files, and the resources you've assembled, you're more focused, efficient, and effective.

To File or Not to File

Why file at all?

Everything you've ever filed presumably had (or has) future value, if only enabling you to cover your derriere:

➤ Files have future value. You file items because you believe that they will come in handy. (You seek to avoid filing items that don't have a future).

➤ There are consequences for not filing. You save receipts from business expenses so you can be reimbursed by your organization and comply with IRS regulations.

If you're in sales, you file information that will enable you to make greater sales in the future. This includes notes on customers and perhaps their catalogs, brochures, and reports.

People often avoid filing because they don't see the connection between filing and its future impact on their careers and lives.

Starting the filing process is time-consuming. However, effective filing saves time later. Rather than spending hours searching for an item, you'll be able to find it—pronto. So it's well worth the time to create a system that supports you.

Pause!
Most of what confronts you will have little impact on your career or your life. Don't let most of what crosses your desk find its way into your files.

Tools to Help Simplify Your Filing Efforts

Filing requires only a few simple tools and the proper mindset. The tools include:

➤ A chair. You can file while standing if you have a four-drawer filing cabinet and you're dealing with the top drawer. Usually, your filing activity is easier if you're in a chair—particularly a swivel chair. If you're way behind in your filing, you won't want to be on your feet.

➤ A desk or flat surface. This comes in handy when you staple or unstaple, paper-clip or un-paper-clip. Often you'll have to mark the folders you insert in your file cabinet, making notes on what you're filing, folding, ripping, or taping together.

➤ File folders. File folders are essential. Rather than the two-cut or three-cut manila folders you can acquire folders in blue, green, brown, red, pink, or black—any color you want. They can be letter-size or legal-size.

➤ File folder labels. These can be color-coded as well. You don't have to order the same old white labels.

➤ Filing cabinets with ample space.

➤ Staplers, paper clips, and other fasteners. Keep these on hand; you never know when you'll need to fasten or unfasten items before you file them.

The Time Master Says

What you file is not etched in stone. You can move things around, chuck them, and add or delete files. Your goal for now is to store items into their best apparent home.

The Value of Establishing a Junk Drawer

Alan Lakein, a noted time management specialist of yesteryear, suggested putting everything that you otherwise can't file right now in what he calls a "C" drawer, meaning it's not an "A" or "B" item. You can't chuck it or deal with it, at the moment.

In this drawer, you temporarily house what you want out of sight and out of mind. Visit your "C" drawer when you have the time (and mental and emotional strength!) to assess the items and determine what needs to go into your file system (probably not much), what you can immediately chuck or recycle, and what goes back into the "C" drawer. I keep a "C" drawer and find it helpful, especially when I'm working on deadline and I encounter something that I don't have time to review immediately. I pop it into the "C" drawer and return to what I was doing.

Pause!

When confronted with too many scraps and information tidbits, it's easy to fall into the habit of parking them in your wallet, on your desk, or in your drawers.

What to Do with All That Paper

When you're confronted by yet another report or document, consider:

➤ What is the issue behind this document? What does the paper represent? Is it an information crutch (data that you already know)? If so, chuck it. Does it represent something that might be important in the future? If so, put it in the "C" drawer.

Often the issue behind the paper flood is, upon reflection, too minor to merit your attention. Sure, it looms large at times, but what doesn't seem important when it arrives in screaming headlines?

➤ Did I need to receive this at all? Often, the answer is no; that means you don't have to spend another second on the item.

➤ How else can this be handled? Can you delegate what needs to be done regarding this new piece of paper? Referring back to Chapter 9, "Buying Yourself Some Time," is someone else in your cosmos capable of handling this and freeing up your time for more important things?

If no one else but you will do, how else can you handle it? Can you pay by check instead of in person? Can you pay by credit card instead of by check? Can you pay online?

Can you highlight the five items in the important company memo that merit discussion at the next meeting instead of trying to comprehend all 22 pages?

➤ Will it matter if I don't handle it at all? Much of what confronts you requires no action on your part. For example: announcements regarding upcoming publications, ads that tout prices or services, and anything addressed to "current resident."

If you don't pay your rent or your mortgage, you'll be contacted by someone interested in collecting the money. If you don't participate in the office pool, don't attend the local charity ball, don't make an extra copy of that recipe, or don't learn about that software game, your life will not change.

Discarding the Discardable

March through your office on a search-and-destroy mission. Round up any suspect that fits these categories and trash or recycle them:

➤ Outdated manuals.

➤ Back issues of publications you haven't touched in more than two years.

➤ Drafts, earlier versions, and outdated versions of letters, correspondence, memos, reports, and documents that have already been produced as final (unless there are legal/financial/tax implications).

➤ All scraps and tidbits of information, used sticky notes, and the like that have accumulated around your desk, in your wallet, and elsewhere. Put them on a single sheet or log them into a file on your computer.

➤ Excess vendor supply catalogs.

➤ Manuals you will never open again.

➤ Outdated catalogs, flyers, reports, brochures, and promotional materials.

➤ The hoard of thumbtacks, pushpins, pennies, and paper clips that gather in the corners of your desk drawers.

➤ Take-out/delivery menus from restaurants you never visit (or visit so frequently that you've memorized the bill of fare).

➤ Lingering stacks of irrelevant documents, and extra copies of relevant documents. Retain what you need. Toss the rest.

Organizing and Filing to Preserve Your Sanity

Suppose you've cleared away excess paper, stashed some items in your "C" drawer, and chucked a variety of other items, yet you still face a build-up on your desk. How would you tackle it? How would you whip that stuff into shape?

Wade through everything rapidly, and determine what can be tossed as well as any duplicate or outdated items you don't need. Some items won't fit in your file folders anyway; it's best to copy the handful of pages you need from them, file those pages, and recycle the rest.

"When in doubt, throw it out." These words, uttered decades ago by efficiency expert Edwin Bliss, are still true. If you're unsure about keeping something, in most cases you've already answered the question: NO. If you're like many professionals, you have a tendency to over-file, which gluts your system and contributes to obscuring anything you need to find.

If you do file too much, use the "C" drawer discussed previously as a pit stop for potential file items.

If you question whether to file an item, put it aside for a day or two and look at it again. Often the answer will emerge. Ask yourself, "What will happen if I pitch this?" If there's no significant downside, chuck it gleefully.

Sort for Similarity

If eight items in your possession refer to delegation, that's a clue to start a file folder labeled "Delegation." Do the same with other groups of like items.

Plow through the entire pile; toss what you can and group like items until everything is tossed or grouped. Yes, some items will stand alone. Not to worry.

When approaching each of your mini-piles, ask yourself these questions:

➤ Can I consolidate each pile by using the backsides of documents, single-page copies, and shorter notes?

Reflect and Win

File folders come in many colors. You can use green file folders for anything that relates to money, red (as in red tape) for government, blue for (true blue) customers, and so on to more easily stay organized.

➤ Can I consolidate scraps and tidbits by using the copier to create a dossier page or stapling them into a packet?
➤ For piles that have only one or two items each, is there a way to group them? (An article on office chairs might join your notes on room dividers in a pile called "Office furniture.")

Maintain Fewer Large file Versus Many Smaller Ones

Review the materials you've put in mini-piles; do any belong in all-encompassing files, such as "Copiers" or "Insurance"? Always seek to have a few large files of like items, not a gaggle of small files. It'll be easier to find what you want in the course of your day, week, year, or career.

Use date-stamping, if it suits you. Some efficiency experts suggest putting a date stamp on every item you file. If you've been holding on to an item for months on end and haven't used it, maybe it's time to chuck it.

It's not mandatory to use date-stamping; an item's future relevance isn't always linked to how long you've had it. Generally, the longer you've held on to an item without using it, the smaller the chance is that it will be of future importance.

Establish File Headings that Convey Meaning

By using customized file headings, you can devise compartments that enable you to give the materials that cross your desk a good home, while you remain anxiety-free, guilt-free, and fat-free.

If you often don't know where to file items, you can create a file called, "Where to file this?" (I use one called "Check in one month.") Other handy file names include these:

➤ Read or chuck
➤ Read when I can
➤ Review for possible linkage with ABC project

Save Time with Tickler Files

You can benefit by creating file folders for each month. Then, when something crosses your desk in December but you don't have to act on it until February, into the February file it goes.

You can have a 31-day tickler file as well. If you receive something on the 2nd day of the month but don't have to deal with it until the 14th, put it in the file marked the 14th—or give yourself some extra time and put it in the file marked the 13th.

Coming to Terms
Tickler files automatically remind you of when you need to deal with a particular task. When the request for the task hits your desk, you can place it in the tickler file for the appropriate future date. Every day of the month, check your tickler file for that day to identify tasks to take on for the day.

You can use this system to pay bills on time when automatic bank drafts or credit card debit options are not available. Write the checks in advance, sign them, seal them, stamp them, and put the envelope in the appropriate folder of your 31-day rotating tickler file. Review that file at the start of each week, and perhaps once or twice during the week; you'll know automatically when it's time to pay a bill or address a date-filed item.

Reduce Clutter through Effective Filing

The monthly files and 31-day tickler files will help you reduce clutter while offering you peace of mind. Simple? Yes. It's also highly efficient.

When you view something several days, weeks, or months after first filing it, you have greater objectivity and a new chance to act on it, delegate it, or toss it. If a lot of stuff is tossed, fine; at least it's out of your system.

Here are some other ways to use your tickler file for timed responses that save you time and help put you on top of things:

➤ Stash tickets to forthcoming events in the appropriate tickler-file date.
➤ Store coupons, discounts, and promotional items until you're ready to use them.
➤ Park items you want to read on your next plane trip in the tickler file for the day before your trip.
➤ Find temporary locations for notes, outlines, and documents you'll want to have on hand when someone visits your office.
➤ Do the same for forthcoming group, department, or company meetings.
➤ Place any mail you receive but choose not to open now in your tickler file; choose a date that seems appropriate for you.
➤ When you're waiting for someone's response, file a copy of your transmission in your tickler file or in a file labeled "Awaiting Response."

Creating Files in Advance of the Need

Suppose you're planning to go to graduate school for a master's degree. One way to accommodate the growing body of literature you'll be assembling is to create a file folder in advance of having anything to file. When stuff comes in that appears worth saving, it'll have a home.

You might think that this is merely a way to collect more stuff. Not! Creating folders in advance of the need can be a potent reminder and affirmation of your future goals.

Suppose you come across a brilliant article on how to finance your degree in a way that considerably reduces your burden. Where are you going to put that article? Park it on top of something else, where it will sit for weeks or months? You still won't know what to do with it, but you'll want to hang on to it—right?

What are some files you can create in advance of having anything to put in them, merely because it makes sense, based on where you're heading in life? Here are some suggestions:

Reflect and Win
You can start a new file folder, label it, and park it in your file drawer without anything in it! Yup.

➤   Your child's higher education fund
➤   Your retirement home
➤   Your vacation next year to New Zealand
➤   Assistance for your aging parents
➤   Evolving technology that interests you
➤   A new medical operation that might affect you

If a new project is about to start, create a directory for it on your hard drive. Suppose Bart is going to start in a few days. The first thing I do is create a directory named "Bart." As the days pass, I move files into Bart's directory so I already have assignments for him. As he takes them on, others develop; I move them to his directory.

I have a directory called "In progress" that I go to at the start of each day; from there I might move an item to "Bart" or (once it's finished) elsewhere on my hard disk. See?

The Time Master Says
At least 50 percent of dealing with all the piles of paper you confront is simply making room for them!

Sheltering Homeless Files

In housing your files, your goal is to keep closest to you the items you use frequently; keep rarely used items farthest from you. Much of what you file won't be used often.

Of course, certain factors—the nature of your work, tax laws, or other regulations—might require you to hang onto more than you'd like. Store whatever you have to hang on to—plus what you want to hang on to—away from your immediate workspace.

Suppose you're hanging onto all kinds of stuff you cannot bear to pitch. Here's a plan of attack:

1. Group like items, put them in a box or storage container, and mark the box with something descriptive, such as "Check again next April," or "Review after the merger."
2. Before storing a container, quickly plow through it once more to see what can be removed. This will simplify your task, and you'll thank yourself later.
3. Once the box is out of sight, build a safeguard into your system. Put a note in your "April" file that says to review the contents of the box located at XYZ.

Sometimes, instead of storing vast volumes of material, you can simply scan it and keep it on disk.

Can anyone else in your organization or family harbor such items so you don't have to? If the box holds reminders of some dear, departed one, perhaps the best solution is to rotate it among the siblings—four months a year at your sister Samantha's, four months at your brother Todd's, and four months with you.

Pay Good Money for Storage

If the stuff you've boxed is valuable and compact, consider a safety-deposit box in a bank. If it's voluminous, put it in a commercial self-storage unit.

Coming to Terms
When you rent a self-storage unit, you are given a garage-like space where you can cram any items you don't need on a daily basis.

Paying to store materials brings up the issue of what you're retaining. Is it worth it to pay a bank or a company to retain the stuff? If it is, then you'll feel all right about forking over the dough. If it doesn't seem worth the cash, you have a viable indicator that you can chuck the stuff.

Winning through Recycling

Watch constantly for what can be recycled. Can you give a report, memo, or article to a key associate or junior staff person whom it will benefit? If so, it's easier to let it go.

Can you use the clean back sides of sheets for rough drafts, scratch paper, internal memos, notepads, and hard-copy fax responses? If so, it will be easier for you to recycle materials that come across your desk. In this case, you're supporting the environment by getting double use out of your materials. All the folders you use are potentially reusable. Label them over again and give them new life. Recycling also gives you a quick and socially acceptable means of dealing with much of the paper and clutter that arrives during the day.

If you don't take control, you're setting yourself up for glutted files, glutted systems, and glutted thinking. Rather than winning back your time, you'll be giving it away. You're at your best when you're a lean, mean, working machine.

CHAPTER 14

Top Time-Management Tools Revealed

In This Chapter:

- ➤ No need for guilt and anxiety
- ➤ Technology time traps
- ➤ Speakerphones, headsets, and two-way recording
- ➤ Simple technologies, affordable prices

This chapter reveals how you can make best use of the tools of technology.

Have you been caught in the trap of gathering information or acquiring an item far in advance of your ability to use it? I'm talking about hardware, software, scanners, additional printers, instruction manuals, adapters, and so on.

Racing Ahead of Yourself?

The only time you have to adopt a new tool or technological device is when: (1) your organization or boss requires it, (2) your clients already use the technology, or (3) you'll gain a strategic competitive advantage.

Peter Drucker, Ph.D., the noted management sage, once made the observation that for new technology to replace old, it had to have at least ten times the benefits of its predecessor. In his book *Technopoly*, Neil Postman, Ph.D., says that the introduction of any new technology into your life brings both benefits and detriments.

The manufacturers, advertisers, and dealers are adept at helping you focus on the benefits—especially in the rare case that you happen to become one of the world's expert users of the system they're offering. How often, however, do you actually read about the

downside of acquiring new tools and
technology in your life?

Some Aspects of Technology are Good, Some Not So Good

Consider the smart phone: by having
the phone in your car, what else have
you added to your life that perhaps you
didn't want? (Note that more than half
of these developments have an impact
on your time.)

Coming to Terms
Technolopy, as Professor Postman
explained it, is the surrender of culture
to technology, at the expense of our humanity and undermining of morality.

➤ The ability of anybody to reach you at any time
➤ Disturbance in one of your last personal sanctuaries
➤ The tremendous potential for driving less safely
➤ The annoying habit of making one extra call before reaching destinations—to make
   sure that plans haven't changed
➤ . . . Thereby leading to heightened insecurity and anxiety
➤ The annoying feeling that your system is insufficient, and that you need more range,
   more capabilities, and lower costs.

It seems paradoxical that a device created to make you more efficient or save you time
holds nearly equal potential for doing the opposite.

Beware of the Revenge Effect

"The Revenge Effect is the curious way the world has of getting even, defeating our best
efforts to speed it up and otherwise improve it," says Professor Edward Tenner of Princeton.
The failure of technology to solve problems, Tenner says, can often be traced to the
interaction between machine and man.

Freeways, intended to speed travel, lead to suburbs—urban sprawl out instead of up,
so commuting times climb. Computers make it easy to copy and print files, so you end up
copying and printing many more files, and your paperless office fills up with paper.

You Need To Make Your Own Rules

You could purchase a smart phone with predetermined rules of use, such as only making
calls to loved ones and for key appointments, limiting calls to less than three minutes, or not
listing your cell phone number on business cards or brochures.

The crucial element is that you define your personal set of rules for using the tool.

Reflect and Win

By viewing each new technological tool as both beneficial and detrimental, you're better able to stay in control of your time.

Rules Related to Making Calls

When you call another party these days, you're subject to endless rounds of voice-mail options. When it's *finally* time to leave a message, ensure that it's sufficiently detailed so that the other person knows specifically why he or she wants to call you back.

Use of the phone is an area ripe with potential savings. Without being short with callers, convey urgency in your voice that lets them know that you're not going to prolong the conversation:

➤ I hear you. I'll report back to you later in the day when I . . .
➤ Gotta run, thanks for keeping me posted.
➤ I'll ponder that one and be back in touch via e-mail.
➤ That's intriguing, but I'm not the right person. Take care.

On personal calls, you have more leeway for deflecting the discussion until later:

➤ You've caught me at a bad time. Can we . . .
➤ Let's talk this evening when I have more time.
➤ I'll catch up with you on the weekend.
➤ I'm knee-deep in paperwork right now, but let's . . .

The Time Master Says

One of the fastest and easiest ways to save your time, and the time of the people you are calling, is to write down a few key words in advance of making a call, perhaps using contact management software with the questions typed into the party's record. By succinctly conveying your message in a minute or two and slowly and clearly stating how you can be reached, you've done yourself and the other party a big favor and saved both of you a lot of time.

Noise Cancellation Technology

Along the same lines of donning a headset, if you fly frequently, consider the new generation of noise-cancellation headphones. They're designed to generate "anti-noise" waves, which neutralize the irritating drone of an airplane engine and surrounding cabin sounds. With fewer distractions, you can accomplish more, and be more in control of your time.

If you fly from New York to Los Angeles non-stop, at flight's end, you'll feel more rested and relaxed. Noise does a number on each of us, often in ways we can't discern. Some models of noise-cancellation headphones allow you to use a two-prong adapter so that you can listen to the in-flight music or programs offered while receiving the benefits of hearing less engine and cabin noise. In fact, you can hear every word of the programs being offered.

Pause!
Noise cancellation headphones do not diminish all noises around you such as people talking to you, a radio, a ringing telephone, or an announcement over a plane's public address system.

Two-way Phone Conversation Recording

Some people use two-way phone conversation recording as a log of conversations to help document highly complex transactions.

Using two-way recording on a personal basis is a marvelous timesaver. As a speaker and author, I find it convenient to be able to record conversations, both ways, with simple, readily available apps. When a meeting planner is giving me essential information over the phone, my ability to capture those words can mean all the difference when it comes to delivering a dynamic program. I cannot take notes as fast as I can capture the meeting planner's words via recording.

Pause!
Detectives, snoops, spies, and our own government have long recorded conversations for purposes of collecting evidence or for entrapment. Clearly, there's a negative connotation to the notion of two-way telephone conversation recording among the under-informed.

When the Conversation Sparks Fly

When I'm interviewing someone for a book, letting other people simply talk—at whatever speed they wish—facilitates effective conversation. The sparks fly. I ask a question, he or she answers. Later, when I review the recording, I am able to glean the essence of what the person said—not what my half-baked notes reveal or my even less effective memory recalls. Often when reporters call me and they're not armed with two-way recording capability, I volunteer to record the conversation for them and email them an MP3.

Reflect and Win

A common misconception about two-way recording is that it's illegal. Not so. You may record any conversation at any time in all 50 States. What's illegal is when neither party knows that the recording is being made. That's called wiretapping or eavesdropping.

The Ethical Question of Phone Recording

While legally you don't have to tell the other party you're recording the conversation, you might feel that ethically it's best to do so. I eliminate this dilemma by simply saying to the other party at the outset, "Do you mind if I record this?" Only a handful of times out of hundreds has anyone said, "I'd prefer not," and I've respected that.

Otherwise, I've been able to capture conversations from mentors giving me advice, peers brainstorming with me on a problem, and the aforementioned meeting planners and journalists.

PART 4

Connecting to the World

Part 4
Connecting to the World

Once you're in charge of your turf—or a least know what it takes to hold your ground—it's time to move into a higher and more efficient gear when it comes to staying in touch with the rest of the known universe. The chapters in Part 4 examine simple to sublime options for staying in touch.

While technology marches forward, each new development isn't always to your benefit. Your quest is to appropriately use or apply the tools and methods of communication discussed here. Otherwise, you might quickly find yourself behind the no-time eight-ball faster than you can say, "The dog ate my homework."

Let's begin with an eye-opening, unnerving, but entirely thoughtful look at a small gadget that can decimate your life (but only if you let it) and turn those all around you into over anxious techno-dweebs.

CHAPTER 15

Staying in Touch Too Much

In This Chapter:

➤ Voluntary versus involuntary gadget enslavement
➤ The Faustian bargain
➤ Keeping in touch, or fanning anxieties?
➤ A negotiable issue

This chapter discusses how too much information and communications impedes our effectiveness, and how, despite the obstacles, you can flourish.

Information overload, not information scarcity, is a problem today for most professionals and leads to mental, emotional, social, and interpersonal issues. For example, while many researchers believe that attention deficit disorder is a biochemical phenomenon, a growing number believe that attention deficit disorder can also be influenced by environmental factors such as the onslaught of too much information. I agree with the second camp.

Interruptions Abound and that is Problematic

Once, the people of the world did not have cell phones. You could attend a movie or a play and not have a patron in the row behind you demonstrate the essence of crassness by checking his phone during the performance.

In the workplace, the typical career professional is confronted by nearly six interruptions every hour!

Personally, in the last five years, every time I give a speech to an audience, whether there are 50 or 500 people in attendance, about 30 minutes into it, somebody's phone sounds. It happens so frequently that I'm used to it, and it neither upsets me nor throws off my timing. I find it curious, however, that someone could sit down to a scheduled presentation of 45 minutes to several hours seemingly oblivious to the fact that his phone might ring.

If you can't control when one of your devices beeps, I wonder, what chance do you have of controlling your time?

Is Constantly Keeping in Touch Too Much?

The prevailing argument is: "If I'm electronically connected to the great mass of humanity at all times, then I can be available when people need me, respond to emergencies, and, in turn be in touch with others when the need arises." It's a Faustian bargain, however, because the price for this sense of security is the elimination of the following luxuries:

➤ Being alone
➤ Dwelling on one's own thoughts without fear of interruption
➤ Working in harmony with one's own internal rhythms
➤ Becoming comfortable, happy, and even content with yourself

Coming to Terms
Shady deals have been called Faustian bargains because the lead character in *Dr. Faustus* by Christopher Marlowe—named Faust, of course—sold his eternal soul to the Devil for a better time on earth.

The typical, yet odd reasoning behind sporting a cell phone, all day long, is to stay connected to others. Is this being connected to others in a meaningful way? Or is it a disguise for individual and mass anxiety?

The need to constantly keep in touch about everything, ranging from the magnificent to the utterly mundane, from that of utmost importance to that which is absurdly trivial, points to a deeper and insidious problem. Over-communication is not necessarily effective communication.

Pause!
Is it any wonder why attention spans have dropped to all-time lows? Is an entire generation doomed to being chained to a cell phone? Will anybody be left who can go for hours—let alone days—without being anxious because they're not "in touch?"

An Electronic Leash even on Vacation

Do you know someone like David, the manager of a sales team for a small food manufacturer? David's company supplied him with a cell phone and a tablet to keep in touch with him on his trips out of town. As a result, even when on vacation, David finds himself connecting with his boss "just to remain in sync."

On a romantic getaway with his wife to St. Thomas, David spends oodles of time in his hotel room instant messaging his boss about an upcoming deal, instead of parasailing or cliff gliding with his wife.

Reflect and Win

In *The Artist's Way*, Julia Cameron recommends that when you're trying to be creative but you feel blocked, rather than being bombarded by the thoughts and words of others, for one week give up reading (except, of course, *this* book), watching television, and listening to the radio. This exercise helps stimulate your own ideas and allows your creativity to emerge.

The following letter, which I received from a man after a speech I gave, is a sad commentary on working in contemporary society:

> *While you were lecturing, my cell phone, pager, voice mail (mental and physical torture device) vibrated no less than three times. Usually I leave the room to listen to the voice mail and return the calls. During your presentation I just let it vibrate. However, I can't turn it off. I carry the phone as a requirement of my job. I must carry it whenever I am officially on the job. Yet, I know peers who are on-call 24 hours to their organizations. They are interrupted by messages at dinners, church, the theater, everywhere.*

If the above scenario even mildly describes your situation, it's time to take control in major ways. If you don't take control, who else on the planet will do it for you?

The Time Master Says
Some theaters in London request attendees to turn off beepers and cell phones before the performance begins. In the U.S., many business establishments, such as restaurants, have strict policies regarding the use of cell phones, with some places regarding them with the same disdain as smoking.

E-Etiquette for Everyone

Dr. Jaclyn Kostner, author of *Virtual Leadership*, advises displaying proper cell phone etiquette:

➤ Turn off your device when attending face-to-face meetings.
➤ Turn off your device during lunch, dinner, or other professional occasions.
➤ Turn off your gadget in nonbusiness public places, such as restaurants, movies, and performances.
➤ Turn off your beeper or cell phone to be with your family and friends.

When to Not Be on Call: Put It in Writing

If your employment is based on a contract—and, often, this is true of top managers and executives—then you have options for not being enslaved by gadgets. When renegotiating your contract, insert a clause allowing for specific times throughout the day or week when you expressly are not responsible for being on call.

If performance reviews and/or appraisals don't occur often enough for you where you work, or if one is not slated until the distant future, arrange a meeting specifically to address this issue.

Depending on how long you've been wearing a pager, how many beeps you receive per day, the nature of your work, and how disruptive the overall effects have been, don't let too many more days

---

Reflect and Win
Whether your employment is based on a contract or not, negotiate to achieve the same results. Whenever it's time for a performance review and appraisal—be it yearly, semi-annually, quarterly, or monthly—discuss with your immediate supervisor the impact on your psyche and physiology of being constantly on-call.

---

or weeks pass before elucidating your views to those who would otherwise have you wear a beeper around the clock and never have another word on the topic.

Energizer Bunny no More!

As tactfully and professionally as possible, inform the powers that be that maintaining ever-ready responsiveness with a pager diminishes your capacity for creativity in those tasks and responsibilities where it's needed.

Pause!
Knowing that any nonwork activity can be disrupted is deleterious to your breathing space. When you can't eat, sleep, make love, or go to the bathroom free of beeper or cell phone-related anxiety, you're not free to live.

The Value of a Message Hierarchy

If most of your messages originate from a central source, such as an executive assistant, instruct that person as to when it's okay for you to be contacted versus not okay. For example, you could use a system as laid out below:

Redirecting Phone Messages

Level 4	Contact me now.
Level 3	Contact me within X hours.
Level 2	Contact me sometime today.
Level 1	No need to contact me at all.

To make this system work, you decide in advance precisely what represents Level 4, so that Level 4 summoning of you is indeed rare. These would be absolute and dire emergencies where your input is absolutely essential. Everything else does not require beeping you every bleeping minute!

Let Lower-Level Issues Wait

Level 1 to 3 issues can wait. Level 3 represents important bits of information but those that are not necessarily urgent. Level 2 represents messages that you could receive at any time during the day because they're not time-related in any way. Most of the messages you receive in a day undoubtedly will fall in this category. Once your assistant becomes adept at recognizing that most messages are Level 2, you'll find you have more stretches of uninterrupted time during the day.

Level 1 represents those messages that fall into the "no need to contact me at all" category. These represent questions that are already addressed by existing printed materials, such as these:

➤ Policies and procedures manuals
➤ Memos
➤ Other items the assistant can retrieve on his or her own

Everyone Working from the Same Page

Admonish the assistant anytime he or she sends a Level 1 message because, indeed, you didn't need to be contacted. You can curtail your assistant's behavior in this category by pointing out, "That was a Level 1 message," whenever you receive one.

Using this system, you'll find that in a matter of weeks—and, more often, in a matter of only days—your assistant will begin to understand with relative accuracy what level to assign to information that potentially could be sent your way.

Start announcing, as well, that such-and-such person can take care of ABC, that you'll be reachable Tuesday from 2 p.m. until 4 p.m., or that the best way to handle JKL problems is to send an e-mail to accounting. In this manner, you might be able to deflect half or more of the messages that would otherwise disturb you.

Also, at certain times on some days, don't carry a cell phone at all, and inform others that you will not be so equipped. Once the umbilical cord is disconnected, certainly your staff and many others learn new ways to proceed on matters without instinctively and incessantly contacting you.

Are You Frequently Sending Messages?

How about the situation where you're supervising others, and you're the one continually sending messages to them so that they're pinged all day long? You've gotten through this chapter thus far, so perhaps you have a newfound appreciation for what you're putting your staff through.

Can you find it in your heart, and does your newfound awareness lead you to the conclusion, that you could be sending fewer messages per day? Chances are highly likely that you could. In most professions, effective managing does not encompass micro-managing around the clock.

If you've selected the right people, trained them accordingly, enabled them to develop on-the-job skills, offered appropriate feedback, made yourself available for coaching, and given them adequate tools with which to perform their assigned tasks, why do you need to be summoning them all day long?

CHAPTER 16

E-Mail
Worse a Curse than Cell Phones

In This Chapter:

➤ Coming at you at high speed
➤ E-mail: not the most urgent thing in the morning
➤ Put spam in its place
➤ To send or to call; that is the question

In this chapter you will learn why email is both a blessing and a curse, and how to make it a blessing more of the time.

Some people check their email two or three hundred times a day! Some incessantly send mail merely to receive mail. Some spend oodles of time actually pondering the legions of spam they receive (see below).

E-mail, along with text messaging and instant messaging, seems to lend itself particularly to various forms of addiction. Still, if you are using it appropriately, it can be useful. How else can you receive a message from somebody or send one to somebody so easily and so quickly nearly anywhere on the globe?

Conversely, the number of e-mails you receive is probably growing at an unwelcome pace.

Pause!
Theoretically, you can become addicted or obsessed with almost anything.

Pause!

It's easy to receive many more e-mails that you can possibly respond to. It's also easy for you to send e-mails to others when no message is needed or wanted. Are you unknowingly glutting the mail inboxes of others? The more you send, the more you receive in return. As a guiding principle, send as few as possible to accomplish your objective and still have a life.

Bamming Spam

We could all use time saving strategies for dealing with spam.

Here are some tips about spam that might help:

➤   If you respond to a spam message by choosing "opt out," you only confirm that there is an actual person behind your email address, which *increases* the amount of spam you receive. Maddening, isn't it? Do not respond to the spammer in any way.

Pause!

It's vital to understand that responding to spam increases the volume of spam you receive. Although it might seem like a good offer, resist the temptation to respond to any spam, even if the feature is to "unsubscribe."

➤   By posting your email address on the Internet through blogs, message boards, directories, and Web pages, you're making it available to spammers. It might also be useful to have a second, more private email account.

➤   Spammers' lists run alphabetically. Since they're often cut off when an ISP notices an attack, addresses at the end of the list often receive less spam than those at the beginning. Therefore, Zach@xdomain.com receives less spam messages than Allyson@zdomain.net

➤   The more complex your email address, the less spam you receive. BillJ@yahoo.com or Quatrina67@Hotmail.com, for instance, will receive more spam than 23rxt98@yahoo.com or dfW32ly668@hotmail.com.

➤   Different Web sites have different policies about the privacy of your email address, so be selective when registering online. When in doubt, don't register.

Beyond the tips above, any time you receive mail that has lots of Xs, all capitals (which is regarded as shouting), or otherwise makes excessive claims, don't waste a nanosecond on it. One writer commented, "You can safely bleep anything that has lots of exclamation marks, assorted promises, and come-ons, or if it looks like it was written by someone who pants for a living."

After accounting for spam, you're still contending with 80 to 120 e-mails per executive per day. In the context of managing your time, keeping your job, and having a life, how do you handle e-mail? Let us count the ways . . .

Perfecting the Art of Subject Lines

If you can't live without listing a subject, wait until you have first composed your message. Then read what you've said, and extract two or three words, making a phrase that you can throw into the subject line. Voilà!

If your e-mail is non-work-related, then you've got it made in the shade. All you have to do in the subject line is put something like _hi, greetings, it's me again, hey, long time_, or something equally harmless. A friend is a friend and is probably glad to hear from you. What does he or she care if you say hi in your subject line? It probably suits your message well, anyway.

Reflect and Win

One study revealed that employees email their coworkers so much and include so many people on their "cc" list, that the result is productivity-sapping. Do you need to cc so many others? Probably not. Likewise you don't need to be on a lot of cc lists.

Serve as Your Own Censor

When you employ the same type of words in your subject heading that spammers use, you run the risk of having your e-mail message being discarded before it's read. Hence, you've lost the time you spent composing the e-mail—and you'll waste yet more time seeking a reply from a party who never read your message to begin with. What are the banished words? You know most of these:

- Sex
- Money
- First time
- Naked

- Free
- Exclusive
- Adults only
- Incredible

- Limited time only
- Don't miss out!
- Make money now
- A one-time offer

Dead giveaways include anything with stars, plus signs, equal signs, or typographical "art work."

Your messages are stored more permanently on an Internet server or network server computer. If you write in disparaging terms about someone else and send it to a third party, expect it to come back to haunt you. If the lawyers come knocking on the door with a subpoena, this is the first place they will look.

The Time Master Says

When compiling e-mail messages that you intend to be read, the most efficient use of your time is to offer a vibrant subject line so that the other party will open and read your mail.

Treat any e-mail you send at work or at home as having the potential to revisit you. If you delete it from your system, it still resides somewhere and the U.S. National Security Agency, among others, can always retrieve it.

Also, unless your job requires continual email monitoring or you're waiting for a critical response, it's best to check your mail only a handful of times per day, *if you possibly can . . .* which leaves out most people.

Pause!

Individuals who are obsessed with checking their e-mail at every spare moment are often the ones not doing a great job anyway.

Online Efficiency through Offline Preparation

The administrivia that you address first thing in the morning, often before downloading new messages, can enhance your productivity in both sending and receiving e-mail. Perhaps you:

➤ need to prepare files on your hard drive.

➤ have addresses to correct.

➤ have received phone messages that will impact your e-mail responses.

Coming to Terms
Administrivia is the irksome and seemingly unending but crucial tasks and details that need to be handled.

I normally start my day at 7:00 a.m. Overall, if I'm free and clear of the morning administrivia and e-mailing before, say, 8:30 a.m., I consider that to be a good start.

I confess to checking after lunch to see if anybody sent me anything, but then I log off rather quickly. I certainly check in at around 4:30 each day, to catch the closing e-mails that might be arriving from East Coast correspondence and from those on the West Coast who know to send their messages in before 2:45 Pacific Standard Time.

Beware of Email's Potential for Miscommunication

Have you ever teed off anyone because of an email? Mere words and letters on a recipient's screen can easily be misinterpreted and, unfortunately, this happens all the time. Did you ever receive a disappointing or questionable email from someone you like?

Sometimes an e-mail message can make you seem curt or abrasive. It's not that you intended to ruffle any feathers; it's that an e-mail message, unless worded carefully, can sometimes come off as impersonal, cold, and uncaring.

Reflect and Win
Michael Eisner, former head of Disney, once said, "E-mail isn't just about speed, efficiency and information. It is also about unscreened emotions, about options untempered by body language, about thoughts unrefined by reflection, about hostility, and provocation. At its worst, it is like talking in the shower with someone listening through the wall."

Pause Before Sending Email

With most providers, you have the option to either park an email message in the "draft message" box or to send it. Too few people apparently are using the draft box and instead clicking the send button nanoseconds after typing the last letter in their message. As with traditional writing, when possible, park emails for a while and revisit them before sending. With some email service providers, you can delay sending until a predetermined time.

When in Doubt, Make That Phone Call

If you rely on e-mail too much—such as sending e-mail when a face-to-face conversation was more appropriate—you might be regarded as somewhat aloof. Managers looking for a way to avoid face-to-face conflict often use e-mail, says Linda Talley, author of *Business Finesse: Dealing with Sticky Situations in the Work Place for Managers.* "It's an easy way out," she says.

If you feel that a conversation is warranted, you're probably right. Make that visit or that phone call. If you need a yes or no answer, or to easily transmit the data that someone has requested or is waiting for, then proceed with e-mail.

Pause!

Don't use e-mail as a substitute for conversation because you will tie up endless amounts of time. It might take a dozen rounds of e-mail for two people to reach the same level of understanding that is possible with two minutes of real-time conversation.

Is Use of Email Warranted?

Everything discussed to this point leads to the inevitable issue: *is the message you wish to convey appropriate via email?* The answer is not always clear. E-mail, like leaving a voice mail message for someone, is a one-way media. When you leave your message, communication is flowing in only one direction. Jaclyn Kostner, Ph.D., president and CEO of Bridge The Distance, based in Denver, Colorado, suggests that these issues are *inappropriate* for one-way media, such as e-mail and voice mail:

➤ The complex
➤ New ideas
➤ Issues requiring clarification
➤ Solicitation for agreement
➤ The emotionally charged
➤ Material that has a strong personal impact on the recipient

Other than what's cited above, it's probably okay to engage in one-way messaging.

Once you've determined that your message is suitable for one-way media, Kostner observes, you have one more choice: to relay your message by e-mail or by voice mail? Let's review her guidelines.

When E-mail is Preferred

Kostner advocates choosing e-mail (not voice mail) when:

➤ When a written record is needed.
➤ Language is a barrier. In multi-language teams, written words are frequently easier to understand than spoken ones, especially when accents are heavy or language skills are less than fluent.
➤ The team's business hours in each location do not match.
➤ You've been unable to reach the person interactively but know the person needs the details right away.

The following also can represent appropriate use of e-mail:

➤ One-word or short answers
➤ Approval or disapproval
➤ Forwarding vital information to appropriate parties
➤ Articles, reports, outlines, and guidelines that have been specifically requested by the recipient
➤ Updated information such as price quotes, progress reports, and summaries, when the other party is expecting or requesting such.

To Be More Effective, Pick up the Phone

Kostner advises leaving a voice mail or answering machine message when your message is urgent or when the recipient is mobile. Voice mail is easier to access than e-mail, in most cases. Also, leave a voice message any time the sound of your voice is key to understanding your message.

CHAPTER 17

Mastering E-Mail So That It Doesn't Master You

In This Chapter:

➤ Skip the preamble and don't ramble
➤ Pruning but not over pruning your messages
➤ Stock messages convey responsiveness
➤ Who is in charge of your email inbox

This chapter offers some sound guidelines for employing email, even if you're a decades-long veteran email user.

Guy Kawasaki, author of *How to Drive the Competition Crazy*, noted that most people send e-mail messages that are too long. Because you're a fast typist doesn't mean you need to ramble on forever. Most of the action is in the first and last paragraphs. If it's longer than four paragraphs, watch out—you're not using the medium for which it was intended, and you're tying up your time.

The Time Master Says

When composing an e-mail message to someone who's not expecting it, but whom you seek to influence, aim for one screenful or less. Imagine that the other person only retrieves email via a smart phone (increasingly true for many people) and craft your message to fit neatly into the allotted space.

Brevity Is the Soul of E-Mail Wit

About those ultra-long e-mail messages you receive: Do you read them all? If you do, how many do you save? Chances are, the longer ones are discarded more quickly.

You can shorten many of your messages, and maybe you already do. If not, start practicing. Prune your prose. Say it once, and be done.

Prune but Don't Over Prune

Occasionally you'll receive an e-mail from someone who uses such cryptic language, chops key words from sentences, and uses many abbreviations. Thus the meaning of the message is all but lost. For example:

looking fw'rd 2 c'ing u this eve. is 7 gd, or do u thk earlier is btr? Also, R U getting tix or me? I'll B in to 5. later, TGB

Don't be among those who prune beyond the recipient's ability to extract

Pause!
Internet abbreviations and emojis are not universally known. When you use such abbreviations, you might confuse the other party, and that's not a time-saver for anyone.

your meaning. You're more likely to confuse the other party than effectively communicate with them.

Reflect and Win
If you tend to include some beginning remark such as "by the way," at the last moment chop it. Your message will read cleaner and neater.

Keep Your "CC's" to a Minimum

Some experts suggest that no more than three parties receive any message that you're sending. So, you'd send to one principal recipient, with circulated copies to two others. If you're the manager of a small group of say ten people, perhaps it's necessary for you to send to all ten. If you're the president of an organization of thousands and you want to send out an all-purpose e-mail to all of them, let 'em rip.

When you CC more than three or four parties in your e-mail for a rather pointed message, you could be signaling to most recipients that they can safely *ignore* your message. As with failure to prune your prose, you're exerting more effort than necessary, such as rounding up more addresses in the CC line and glutting other peoples' e-mail inboxes. You don't want to do that, do you?

Achieve a True "Net" Savings

If you prune your prose effectively, email can remain a valuable tool. After all, even if you're inundated with email messages, a net time savings accrues in the form of less mail, and fewer telephone calls (hopefully) from these same parties.

If you productively handle your e-mail, you effectively reduce the time and tasks associated with other forms of correspondence.

Showing Your Responsiveness

With a multitude of e-mail messages piling up, even a brief time away from your PC or phone means you'll have scads of e-mails to respond to upon returning. You can let the build up drive you crazy, or you can practice triage.

Practice Triage or Die

I advocate practicing triage for all email messages, all the time. First, quickly eliminate the inane. These include all forms of spam.

After eliminating the obvious, the next question is which e-mails could you park, for now. Some messages are worth saving but are not urgent. Some are from friends and loved ones, and you want to pore over what they've written. Some have told you in their message that the reply time need not be immediate.

Coming to Terms
Triage is the practice of quickly poring over a variety of items and allocating them based on what needs to be handled now, what can be handled later, and what can be ignored.

Those e-mail messages that merit a reply—right now—while you're online, hopefully, are small in number.

For those e-mails that mandate your earnest and rather speedy attention, do your best to handle them so that they're sent, and you're mentally clear of them.

Reflect and Win

If a message is not urgent, but you're able to respond to it quickly and effortlessly then handle it then and there.

Make Stock Messages for All Occasions

If the number of email messages in your inbox is rising, have stock messages ready, such as, "I have recently returned from traveling and will respond by mid-week," or anything else that conveys your sense of responsiveness.

When I receive an acknowledgment message from someone (even an automated acknowledgment), I regard that person favorably. He let me know that he received my message and intends to do something about it. That's a far cry from those you don't hear from for days, much of the time suspecting that you'll never hear from them.

Delegate When You Can

Among the *important* emails you receive, if you're a manager, you'll have support staff to manage, delegate and forward many of your email messages to your staff. If you're not delegating email, you're holding on to too much!

Not delegating has cost many executives a vital promotion and, worse, has led some to the unemployment line.

Pause!

You can rationalize about how much you accomplish in a day and the wonderful things you do that aren't counted. Still, reading, composing, sending, and filing email that isn't work related means that you are dawdling on the job.

Pssst . . . Don't Pass it On

Do you forward semi-amusing jokes or email chain letters? The stories that you hear about people winning riches are baloney.

Any type of dawdling when it comes to email is a time waster. When you dawdle in the office, repercussions ensue, and *extensive* use of the phone, email, voice mail, or text mail for personal reasons steals time from your employer.

If you're on commission, you have a stronger argument that how you use your time is up to you. The larger question is what else could you be doing with this precious time?

Working Offline to Increase Your Productivity Online

While in some professions checking email first is mandatory, many professionals have the option of checking email when they choose. Here's the case for *not* emailing until later in the morning.

When you log on first thing in the morning, you're automatically compelled to pay attention to what's new, current, or tugging at your time and attention. Whatever you had planned for the day could take second place to tasks you feel obligated to perform as a result of the emails you received. This is not to say that you are not receiving important emails requiring timely turnaround.

The question becomes which is more vital: to proceed based upon your personally crafted agenda or the one that transpires as a result of being hit by many emails?

Take an Offline Look

When I start work, I review email from previous days that I have saved and arranged in various files and folders. Then I compose letters offline and put them into the "drafts" folder. I send it when I'm ready, not in a rush.

Much of what I receive consists of items that I wish to copy and move into my word processing software because they are worth retaining. I move at my own pace.

I examine emails that I didn't know what to do with the first time around. Sometimes I delete them. Some I file for future examination. Most, I deal with then and there, formulating replies and saving them in the drafts pile.

Ready to Go Online

Because I have not allowed myself to be besieged by all types of new messages, I'm in a more commanding position to take action as I see fit and stay in control of my time and my day.

Coming to Terms

Formulating an email reply is different that simply responding to one. It entails ensuring to the best of one's ability that the message is clear, accurate, and conveys precisely what the sender wishes to communicate.

Receiving Before Sending

Before sending my drafted letters to their intended recipients, I press "Get Messages." Sometimes the messages received supersede the messages I was ready to send to someone. A new message might resolve the issue all together. As the new emails appear on my screen, I review them, then I turn to my draft files and launch the email in waiting.

Because I logged on later in the morning after handling my existing email files, purged the spam, handled the quick reply messages, and filed the information I wished to retain on my hard drive, I am usually left with only a handful of pressing tasks. This approach helps me stay in balance, feel in control, and offer a high level of attention to the remaining emails that merit an extended effort.

In situations that might take a while to resolve, I sometimes send a stock message or short note back to the sender saying, "I'm working on it, and will be back in touch on such and such day." This lets the sender know that I received the message and, while I can't resolve the issue or meet the request at that moment, I certainly am working on it.

The Elements of Effective Online Management

Being effective requires an understanding of how you work best, what will help you to maintain control, and what yields the greatest productivity.

Here are some additional components that might aid in your overall work effectiveness:

➤   Create an online file folder for each of your major projects and for each broad topic important in your work and your life, such as "work," "family," "school," and so on.

➤   Establish a variety of folders on a temporary basis, when an issue or project is at hand, and eliminate the folder when the significance of the issue recedes.

➤   Use filters to eliminate spam and other types of messages that you don't want to receive, as well as messages from certain senders. The less unwanted email messages you see, the more effective you'll be at handling all else.

➤ Employ a template, which is a pre-written response, when you have to give the same answer more than a few times, or to disseminate a message to several recipients. You can always eliminate templates that are no longer useful to you. It's better to create a template and not use it than not to create one and have to repeat entering the same type of message over and over again.

➤ When you encounter a useful web address, but find you don't have time to visit it right then, send yourself an email containing the address.

At all times, you're in charge of your email; it is not in charge of you. By using the techniques above, email need not be the burden that many career professionals perceive it to be.

Reflect and Win

Because you can rename, combine, or submerge folders easily, and because the nature of your work is probably dynamic, it makes sense to move folders, in some way, at least once a week. If you are not doing so, chances are, you're not using email as effectively as you could.

Ready for Action

If any incoming emails contain vital information in the message section or attachment, I copy the information, then wheel over to my contact management software and place it in the record of the person who sent me the information.

For example, if Ryan sends me an important list via e-mail, I copy that list then put it in my database file under "Ryan." If I need to insert the list into a report, I copy and paste it into my word processing software.

By cutting and pasting from one window to the next as necessary, I'm able to:

➤ Stay in touch with parties in an efficient manner
➤ Keep my email in-box relatively clear
➤ Maintain an easy way to find information sent to or from specific parties
➤ Maintain peace of mind

Thinking Your Way Out of Time Traps

Part 5
Thinking Your Way Out of Time Traps

Thus far we've covered leaving the office on time, understanding why time flies, and recognizing that we're all in the same boat, as well as identifying priorities and supporting goals, seeking help, and getting more sleep. We've also addressed volunteering a little less, whipping your office and files into shape, using time-enhancing tools profitably, and examining how and when you communicate with others.

None of the individual changes suggested were too huge, but they do require concerted effort. By contrast, the tips and recommendations in the next few chapters require *less* work!

CHAPTER 18

Decide or Let It Ride

In This Chapter:

➤ Choices and resulting decisions you'll face

➤ Refraining from making a decision

➤ More data can be confounding

➤ Using the power of your intuitive abilities

If it feels like it's getting harder or taking longer to make an effective decision, this chapter if for you.

On a planet of Seven plus billion people, volumes of information are being generated and are sped your way by worldwide media. The more information you're exposed to, the more choices you face and the greater the unrelenting pressure on you to choose. Any way you cut it, you're confronted by too many decisions—at work, at home, on the weekend, while traveling, when you wake, when you retire at night, and even when you're on vacation.

Choices and Needed Decisions on the Rise

Society spews information in abundance. When you go to the drug store to buy something as inconsequential as shampoo or skincare lotion, beware. More than 1,200 varieties of shampoo and more than 2,000 skincare products are on the market. Choices abound in other arenas as well. At least 3,000 books are published in the United States each week. Ten times as many radio stations exist today than when television was first introduced.

The level of bombardment has passed the point where anyone can absorb even a small fraction of what he or she has encountered. In his 1969, landmark book *Future Shock*, Alvin Toffler said that in the future too many choices will compete for your time and attention. He was right. Manufacturers, using mass-customization, offer you products with whatever bells and whistles you want (along with advertisements that make you want them).

Meanwhile you're besieged by too much information—much of it conflicting—and the onslaught impedes your ability to choose. To win back more of your time, identify the big decisions and make them quickly. Start by determining which decisions are worth making and which are worth forsaking.

Worth Making, not Forsaking

Recall Chapter 7, "What Matters Most to You?" and Chapter 8, "Sustaining Your Priorities for Fun and Profit" and the discussion on establishing priorities and goals. What you establish as important in your life links directly with decisions that are worth making.

Many people mix decisions worth making with those worth forsaking, treat them almost equally, and wonder where the time went. When a choice will significantly impact one of your life's priorities, that's a decision worth making.

If your boss requests that you make a decision, the situation is clear-cut. Still, decisions worth making are often conditional. If you're single and trying to choose between two likely partners, your decision will affect the quality of your life in the foreseeable future, and perhaps the rest of your life. The following are examples of decisions worth making:

➤ The choice of a spouse
➤ The choice of a home
➤ Major work decisions your organization requests of you
➤ Where you'll live
➤ With whom you'll associate
➤ What course of study you'll pursue
➤ Whether you wish to climb to the top of your organization or profession

Decisions worth making, while often conditional, are not always apparent. Consider the following five issues. Are they decisions worth spending any time on? It all depends. In the list that follows, mentally circle the decisions you believe worth making:

➤ The color of the next toothbrush you buy
➤ The next movie you see
➤ Whether to attend the next PTA meeting
➤ Whether to take your car in for a tune-up tomorrow
➤ What to eat for breakfast

Have you finished circling the items above? So what are the right answers? As you might have guessed, there are none.

Choices Worth Forsaking, Not Worth Making

Decisions worth forsaking are plentiful. When you're faced with too many decisions in general, your reflex action is likely to be an attempt to grapple with all decisions.

1. The color of the next toothbrush. For most people this is a decision worth forsaking; it can't be that important. When might it be? If the decor of your home and bathroom is of utmost importance to you (it is for some people), then this becomes a decision worth making.

2. The next movie you see. It's likely you only go to movies you think you'll enjoy; when you see one you don't like, it is a mistake, but the earth doesn't tremble. If you consider movies as pure leisure, then which one you see is not vital. Of the hundreds of movies you've seen in your life, how many have had a significant, lasting impact on your actual behavior and activities?

When would it be? If improving the cultural component of your life, is among your priorities, and the movie is of the slasher variety, your decision is clear: don't go see it. If attending a movie with your kids, then, obviously, you are bound to make a more thoughtful decision.

3. Going to the next PTA meeting. Your child's education or the betterment of your community is likely a high priority, so you would attend. If your child is doing extremely well in school, or if you're pleased about the school system in general, you could skip one meeting or even a run of them.

4. Do you need to put your car in the shop tomorrow? Has your car been running poorly lately? What is the cost of being tied up on the highway and not arriving at work on time, and causing 10,000 people to snarl at you? Can you bring work with you to the repair shop, or can they give you a ride back to work quickly after your arrival? Is preventive maintenance part of your overall plan to be ready and stay on top of things? The more people who take care of their automobiles, in advance of any failure to perform, the fewer breakdowns on the highway. This is good for everyone.

5. What to eat for breakfast. If you're already 32 pounds above your ideal weight and have no resolve for getting back into shape, what you eat for breakfast tomorrow morning matters less than the longer-term health concerns you're facing. Go ahead and eat that honey-glazed doughnut with your coffee. If becoming the first octogenarian to visit the moon is a priority for you, your choice is clear: go healthy.

What represents a low-level decision? When a coworker asks you where you want to go to lunch today, your response will most appropriately be, "You decide." Of the couple thousand times you've been to lunch, can you recall any significant impact related to your decision on where you went? One day maybe you met somebody you started dating. Another time, you learned something new. Another time you got heartburn. In general, one single lunch doesn't have much impact.

Examples of decisions worth forsaking include these:

> ➤ The park where you'll take your children to play; given that two parks are equally safe, and nearby, let them decide.
> ➤ Whether to catch the news at 10 p.m. or not.
> ➤ Whether to buy Del Monte or Bird's Eye frozen vegetables.
> ➤ Whether to visit Colorado for five days or six.

> **Coming to Terms**
> A low-level decision carries few or no significant consequences, whatever decision you make. Don't waste time agonizing over low-level decisions—you have better things to do.

Are there any perceptible benefits to making fewer choices per day? Yes! When you attend a dinner party and the host has already assigned seating to the guests, it's an act of kindness. It reduces anxiety about who'll be in the chair beside you. This is a time-honored tradition from Walnut Creek, California, to the White House.

When Stuck, Action is Invigorating

If you find yourself over-analyzing situations, relent. You've been trained from birth to collect all the data, statistics, articles, reports, and information you could gather before making a decision that involves the outlay of any sizable sum.

When two groups of executives had to make a large purchase decision for their respective companies, the first group was armed with information—reports, data, and statistics. Understandably, they used whatever information they could to make the purchase decision.

The second group consisted of individuals who had no such data or statistics. They used instinct or intuition alone.

Weeks after the purchases had been made and everyone got to see the results, which group do you expect was happier with its decision? If given a

> **Reflect and Win**
> Much of the data you collect could be redundant, reaffirming what you already know. Too often, you unconsciously collect information that supports what you already know or believe.

chance to be in one group or the other, you would have chosen to be in that well-informed group. So how is it that the second group was happier with their decisions?

If you're 30 or 40 or 50 years old, everything you've learned in your life up to now is summoned when you make a decision. There's far more to instinct or intuition than is generally acknowledged.

Traps in Collecting Data Lie in Waiting

Traps await in collecting data on the way to making a decision. The more data you collect, the likelier it is you'll get conflicting answers.

Sometimes the data that you collect is nothing more than a crutch. Or sometimes its only purpose is to cover your derriere (if the decision turns out unfavorably), by having an authority to cite: "It says right here blah, blah, blah."

Sometimes the data you collect is a substitute for taking action. Studying a decision is a classic way to delay making it. (The government has done it for years.) In all cases, whatever data or information you collect has to be applied.

More Data, more Hesitancy?

More data is not always the answer, but what's the alternative? I'll deal with intuition in a moment. For now, here are some techniques for making big decisions in record time and deriving the answers you want with less effort:

➤ Three calls away from any expert. If you can identify the single best person to call to start off your information search, you can obtain your answer within two more calls. Who's the first person to call? It could be your municipal or college library, an expert you found on line, an official of an industry or professional association, or an information service firm (such as market researchers). Perhaps you can find an expert within the government, or an editor at *Consumer Reports.*

➤ Finding the trailblazer. Have others already made a decision like this? If so, and if their circumstances are somewhat similar to yours, learn what they have discovered. Network with people in your field and tap them for their experiences as needs arise.

➤ Consensus building. Can you assemble a group, hash it out, and base your decision on the consensus reached? Often, this works fine.

➤ The answer will simply emerge. This alleviates a lot of decisions. As circumstances unfold, often the decision that makes the most sense becomes apparent. If you suspect this might be the case, and you have some slack, sit back and let time take its course.

Decisions Disguised as Problems

Many decisions that you have to make are designed to solve problems. Problems often can be approached productively when you see them as opportunities or challenges. In The *Path of Least Resistance*, Robert Fritz suggests that you view problems as your best friends.

How does facing a problem help you reach higher ground? This view of problem solving works best when you're not dealing with extremes—neither a hangnail nor the death of a loved one.

If the decision you face is a disguised problem, try treating it as your best friend or a teacher with wisdom to impart. You might dislodge something in your decision-making process and proceed more easily.

Biographers have noted that Ben Franklin listed the pluses and minuses of one path versus another when faced with big decisions. Sometimes he gave weight to them; sometimes he didn't. Listing your potential options on paper or anywhere else for that matter, still beats merely weighing them in your mind. Also, you can keep better track of them this way.

Reflect and Win

If you derive a decision that addresses the immediate situation *and* provides long-term benefits, then you've got something.

In *Feel the Fear and Do It Anyway*, Dr. Susan Jeffers suggests that when you face a decision that represents a hurdle or a roadblock, let yourself feel all the emotions that arise. Are you uneasy? Quivering? Light-headed? Is your stomach upset, are you trembling, or do you feel fearful?

When you're honest with yourself about how you feel (namely, scared), initiate your decision anyway, Jeffers says. Often you're able to break through your fear and overcome the obstacle that loomed so large when you weren't being honest with yourself.

Listen to Your Inner Voice

The fastest way to make decisions is to use your instincts or intuition. You're already good at this; you got this far in life.

Write down your intuitive choice before making any final decision. Then, when enough time has passed to see the results of a more analytical decision, write them down and compare them to the results of your intuitive choice. As time passes, you'll notice how frequently your intuitive choices were wise ones and find yourself trusting your hunches more easily and more often.

The Time Master Says

When you become adept at trusting your intuition, you can bypass reams of data and information that might have impeded your ability to choose. You can call upon your still, quiet, and faithful internal guidance system.

More than Throwing Darts: Intuition in Action

How did you select your dentist? Did you go online or open up the phone book and collect the names of the ten, 11 to 12 dentists nearest you, then call each of them, decide (based on the call) to visit five to seven, visit their offices, grill each one on billing procedures, background, expertise, competency of their staff, office hours, prices, and overall philosophy? Then did you whittle down the list to maybe two or three, call them back or visit on another occasion, and do some background checking for reputation, longevity in the community, and professional standing? Then, and only then, did you decide on a dentist?

Or did you choose a dentist on the basis of who your parents or friends see, where a referral service sent you, or simply a clever flyer you saw? You probably employed a combination of references and intuitive processes to choose your dentist.

Why, then, do you over-complicate many decisions at work and in the rest of your life?

Using Every Single Shred of Intelligence

When you base a choice on intuition, every cell in your body and every shred of intelligence you've ever accumulated are brought to bear. Much is occurring to reach the choices you make.

New information will hit you faster and faster as your life proceeds. You'll be able to absorb and apply only a fraction of what you encounter. When you have no time for exhaustive research on a consumer product, trust your instincts.

Pause!

Pay attention to your small voice. That's your intuition talking, and it will support you if you listen to it.

Making a Real World Decision

Suppose you're considering whether to move to town A or town B. What factors would you logically consider?

➤ Housing prices
➤ Taxes and demographics
➤ Schools
➤ Crime
➤ Community groups
➤ Family and friends
➤ Lakes, streams, and beaches
➤ Trails and mountains
➤ The business community
➤ Population density
➤ Education levels
➤ Nearby colleges
➤ Churches, synagogues, and mosques
➤ Road systems
➤ Major highway access
➤ Shopping
➤ Traffic patterns

Dozens of factors could be analyzed and compared. In the end, your decision would probably be based on some combination of data (though not too much) and intuition (probably a lot).

Procrastination is a Temptress

When faced with many decisions, your natural inclination might be to procrastinate. Relatively easy decisions become more involved when there's too much on your plate. Here's how to overcome procrastination that stymies your decision-making process:

➤ Ponder what is actually blocking you? What is the real reason you don't want to choose? Write it down or record it. This exercise alone could help you decide.
➤ Choose to easily begin. Make a positive affirmation of yourself: "I can easily make this decision." This affirmation has power and is often enough.
➤ Find the easy point. Ask yourself, "What are three to five things I could do to progress toward the final decision without actually tackling it head-on?" Then initiate these "easy entry" activities. Often, they're enough to get you fully involved.

➤ Set up your desk or workspace to focus on the decision at hand; ignore other (less important) matters.

Most of your decisions will have only a minimal impact on your life; don't let the fear of being wrong shackle you unduly.

For Purchase Decision, Use a Good Set of Questions

When you need to make a purchase decision, sometimes all you need is a good set of questions to ask. Here's a checklist of questions for making sound purchase decisions more quickly:

➤ Are there quantity discounts or special terms?
➤ Are there corporate, government, association, or educators' discounts?
➤ Do they give weekly, monthly, quarterly, or seasonal discounts?
➤ Do they give off-peak discounts or odd-lot discounts?
➤ Do they offer a guaranteed lowest price?
➤ Do they accept major credit cards?
➤ Do they accept orders by fax? By e-mail?
➤ Do they offer a money-back guarantee or some other guarantee?
➤ Do they have a toll-free ordering line and customer service line?
➤ Do they guarantee the shipping date? How do they ship?
➤ Do they offer free delivery? Free installation?
➤ Will they keep your name off their mailing list (unless you want to keep up with special sales)?
➤ Do they intend to sell, rent, or otherwise transfer your name and ordering information to others?
➤ Are their shipments insured?
➤ Are there shipping and handling charges? Are their prices guaranteed? Is there tax?
➤ Are there any other charges?
➤ Do they have free samples?
➤ Are authorized dealer/repair services in your area?
➤ Are references or referral letters available?
➤ Are there satisfied customers in your area?
➤ How long have they been in business?
➤ Whom are they owned by?
➤ How long for delivery?
➤ Is gift-wrapping available?
➤ Does the product come with a warranty?

CHAPTER 19

 # Concentration:
A Largely Lost Art

In This Chapter:

➤ Does doing several things at once "save" time?

➤ Doing one thing at a time and doing it well

➤ Sticking with the task at hand

This chapter discusses why, in a society where others seem hell-bent on providing an endless round of distractions, if you can hone and refine your powers of concentration, all other things being equal, you'll do a better job and have more time at the end of the day.

Focusing on the task at hand and giving it your full concentration, yields high productivity. As cited in Chapter 7, the importance of concentration and focus cannot be understated.

A friend of mine has a saying that is appropriate here: "Focus trumps brilliance each time."

Multitasking is Risky Business

People attempt to do too much at one time. Whether they're at home, at work, or driving in their cars, too many people resort to multitasking to complete tasks.

Does multitasking enable people to accomplish more? Research shows that the opposite might be true! A study published by *American Psychological Association's Journal of Experimental Psychology: Human Perception and Performance*, conducted by researchers Joshua Rubinstein, Ph.D., David Meyer, Ph.D., and Jeffrey Evans, Ph.D., found that the effects of multitasking can actually be counterproductive.

"People in a work setting, who are banging away on word processors at the same time they have to answer phones and talk to their co-workers or bosses—they're doing switches all the time," says Meyer. Not being able to concentrate for, say, tens of minutes at a time might mean it's costing a company as much as 20 to 40 percent of its income. The researchers refer to this cost as "time cost."

"In effect," Meyer says, "you've got writer's block briefly as you go from one task to another. You've got to

a. make a decision to switch tasks,
b. actually make the switch and then,
c. warm back up to what you were doing."

Coming to Terms
Time cost, or efficiency cost, is the time you lose by switching from one task to another

The Detrimental Effects of Multitasking

The effects of multitasking could be detrimental to more than your job. You might be putting yourself, and others, in danger by performing too many tasks at once.

For many years, I've been an avid reader of *Men's Health,* and I greatly look forward to each new issue. One article from the late 1990s titled "Dining a la Car" discussed clever ways to eat while driving. It was among the poorest ideas they've presented. Eating while driving is dangerous.

Pause!
Talking on a cell phone while driving, for instance, might seem safe enough, but you do not realize how much attention it requires.

You Can't Have It Both Ways

"A lot of folks," says Meyer, "think, 'Well, cell phoning while driving is no big deal and I can get away with it.' Even if you have hands free cell phone capability and can dial by voice, you still have a big conflict." When you're driving you need to look different places, read signs, and make decisions about where to go. You cannot be at your best while on the phone because you "have to use your 'inner ears' and 'inner speech' and even your 'inner eyes' to imagine what the person on the phone is talking about."

The same study also shows that the "costs" of multitasking increase with more difficult tasks. "A very simple conversation on the phone while driving a car—'Honey, please pick up some bread on the way home'—might not draw too much concentration," Rubinstein says, "But if the conversation becomes difficult or emotionally charged or mentally taxing—like 'Honey, the house is burning down, what should I do?'—it draws more attention and more mental resources away from your primary task, which is driving the car: you're more likely to have an accident."

Pause!
Kids are attempting to do too many things while they do their homework and it's decreasing the quality of their work.

Curbing the Urge to Multitask

As people become more available by phone, email, and other means of communication, they feel as if they're always "on alert," a situation that can become mentally exhausting.

Reflect and Win
Computers are equipped to handle more than one task at a time. Human beings are not computers, no matter what analogies or metaphors you might have read or heard.

It's easy to fall into a familiar trap: "So much is expected of me, I have to double and triple my activities."

Messages in society imply that it's okay—or necessary—to double or triple the number of activities you perform at once.

Consider Bob W., age 44, who works for a large brokerage firm in the International Square building in Washington, D.C. He is friendly, successful, and always in a rush. He talks fast, moves fast, eats fast, and never lets up. Bob is hooked on multitasking. Many executives and career-climbers suffer from a misdirected sense of urgency stemming from far too many tasks and responsibilities. Certainly, it's appropriate to work more quickly than normal at certain times. Working hurriedly is a problem when it becomes a standard operating procedure.

Pause!
At the workplace and at home, attempting to multitask ensures that you'll miss your day, week, and ultimately your life. People who are 40 years old can't remember where their 30s went, and people who are 50 can't remember where their 40s went.

Reflect and Win

When you undertake original or creative thinking—work with numbers, charts, or graphs; or write, copy-edit, or proofread—put aside all other tasks until you've finished. Diverting your attention results in less than your best effort; often it leads to costly errors.

Unnecessarily Overtaxing Your Brain

The psychic toll you place on yourself in attempting multitasking (or in doing one stressful job for too long) can be harmful. Your brain can become overtaxed! Job related stress accounts for most of the absenteeism and illness that the typical professional today experiences. At least one in four professionals contends with anxiety-related illness.

Consider air-traffic controllers who have been on duty too long, had too many planes landing at a given time, and are responsible for safekeeping hundreds by making the right decisions with split-second timing. It's no wonder that this is a high-stress, high-burnout position, one that professionals usually abandon at a young age.

Pause!

The false economy of attempting to do two things at once is ingrained in a culture that rewards 16-hour-a-day entrepreneurs, workaholics, supermoms, and hyper-energetic students.

Be Effective, Never Mind Being Busy

Researchers at the Medical College of Wisconsin have discovered if you perform a task as simple as tapping your foot, you activate the primary motor in your cortex, a section of your brain. If your task is more involved, if it includes planning to tap your foot to a sequence (such as one-two, one-two-three, one-two, one-two-three), then two secondary motor areas in the front of the cortex are engaged. You are drawing upon more of your brain's functioning capacity.

Don't worry. Your brain can handle it. The point is that when you engage in multitasking—such as attempting to watch TV while eating, or doodling while you talk on the telephone—your brain functioning changes to incorporate the extra activities.

To do the best at whatever you're doing, allow your brain to concentrate on one activity—focus on one thing at a time.

I sometimes conduct a brief exercise with my audiences when speaking at conventions and executive retreats. I ask audience members to take out their watches or cell phones and do nothing but stare at them for a solid minute. Few can do it! In this society, you're fed a message that emphasizes the importance of motion and activity. Merely reading, thinking, or reflecting doesn't look busy enough.

The Time Master Says

"Men give me some credit for genius. All the genius I have lies in this: When I have a subject at hand I study it profoundly. Day and night it is before me. I explore it in all its bearings. My mind becomes pervaded with it. Then the effort which I have made is what people are pleased to call the fruit of genius. It is instead the fruit of labor and thought."

—Alexander Hamilton

When Doing Nothing Pays Off

Has the following happened to you? Somebody walks by your desk and, horror of horrors, you're reading! Maybe you receive a funny look or experience guilt feelings because you're not "in motion." Yet studies show that informed people in executive positions read two to four hours each day.

To be as productive as you need to be, you often need to act in ways that run counter to what society tells you is "productive activity." To reach your full potential, you've got to break out of the mind-set imposed by others.

Sometimes the best way to be productive is to sit and do nothing: at least nothing that looks like anything to people walking by. Reading or staring out the window in contemplation could be the most important activity you do in a day.

What happens when you jump between different projects? It might feel "dynamic"—after all, you're exerting lots of energy. Yet there's a loss of productivity. You and a friend can test this easily at your desk or table.

Reflect and Win

Too often, you probably throw your time at tasks when first you need to reflect on them.

Try This Exercise at Home

Decide on any three minor tasks that the two of you can do simultaneously. One task could be stacking pennies; another could be drawing 15 stars on a sheet of paper; a third could be linking paper clips. You each have the same number of items.

You and your friend start these tasks at the same time. You stack a few pennies at a time, make a few stars on a piece of paper, and link some paper clips, randomly alternating between the three tasks.

Meanwhile, your friend stacks all the pennies to completion until there are no more. Then (s)he turns to drawing stars on a page and reaches 15. Finally, comes linking the paper clips, until they're all linked.

Who do you think will finish faster and easier, and be in better shape mentally and emotionally? Your friend, who focused on the task at hand, took it to completion then turned to the next one while you were bouncing back and forth between activities. You might have been more prone to errors, such as knocking over one of your stacks of pennies. Even if you were quite an adept task-juggler, you couldn't keep pace, or the quality of your work was not as good. Perhaps your paper clips became tangled, or your 15 stars lacked artistic merit.

Multiply the effect of this test by how often you flip-flop between activities in a day or a year, and it's easy to realize why you're losing productivity. Continually switching tasks is not as productive as staying on one job until completion.

CHAPTER 20

Dare to Focus

In This Chapter:

➤ You can manage the distraction
➤ Your own interruption-management system
➤ Concentration on the fly

This first of two short chapters in a row highlights the benefits of learning how to become more focused. For today, give yourself the benefit of working on one thing at a time. You might have to switch gears when that important phone call comes through, when the boss summons you, or if you receive a message that has to be handled right away.

Offer Your Complete Attention

When you switch gears, switch them entirely: give your complete and undivided attention to the pressing issue at hand. You'll likely find that this is a more enjoyable, more effective way to work.

If you notice yourself gravitating toward multitasking, try these solutions:

➤ Take a 15-minute break once during the morning and once in the afternoon. That also means don't eat at your desk: depart to "recharge your battery."

Coming to Terms
To gravitate is to move towards or be attracted to.

➤ Invest in equipment or technology that offers you a notable return—it pays for itself within one year or less, or it saves at least two hours a week of your time.

➤ Hold regular meetings with your team to discuss how everyone can be more productive without multitasking. Focus on the big picture of what you're all seeking to accomplish. Often, new solutions to old problems will emerge, and activities that seem urgent can be viewed from a broader prospective.

➤ For a more human workplace, furnish your office with plants, pictures, art, or decorations that inspire creativity.

Reflect and Win
When facing several projects, begin working on the most important one until its completion, then go on to the next project, and then the next, until you are finished.

When you're feeling overwhelmed or time-stressed, ask yourself who created this situation. Often you'll discover that you did. Of course, sometimes the boss lays a bombshell on your desk and you're asked to do more than usual. It's your responsibility, still, to tackle this challenge. Acquire resources, training, or know-how that enables you to handle tasks that come your way.

A Systematic Approach to Minimizing Interruptions

Author Alvin Toffler once said to me that the traditional workplace is a terrible place to get things done. With the distractions in your office, it's often better to work at the library, in the conference room, or on a park bench. This is especially true when you're doing conceptual or breakthrough thinking, when you need to have quiet space.

Years back, I was consulting for a supervisor in Minnesota with six employees; he wanted to use his time productivity. He said his staff members came to him with questions every couple of hours. That seemed harmless enough, but if someone asked him a question every two hours, with six employees, that meant 24 questions a day, or 120 interruptions each week.

I devised a system to help him with the interruptions and regain control of his time: I called it the "J-4 System." The J was for Jeff. You can use your own initial. The system works in a similar way to how you fend off too many email messages (see Chapter 16.)

I had the supervisor put the questions into four categories of manageability. The first level of distraction, a J-1 type, represented something that was already answered in print and did not need a personal reply (ie. it was in the company policy manual or FAQs). The supervisor was then able to tell his employees, "Please don't bother me with J-1 distractions."

The second level of distraction, J-2, was a question that a peer or bookkeeper could answer; the supervisor did not need to be bothered with this type of question either.

A J-3 distraction needed only a short answer, usually a yes or no. Such questions required interaction with the supervisor, but not much: a quick phone call, or text message or IM. The final category, J-4 distractions, required the supervisor's response.

How many questions were at the J-4 level of importance? Even assuming each person asked two J-4 questions per day—60 interruptions each week—this would cut the number of interruptions in half! Almost immediately, the supervisor was able to better use his time and reduce his level of stress.

You're likely to face more distractions in the future, not fewer. To regain control, handle distractions in new ways. With the J-4, you'll gain greater control over your work, find more time, and feel more relaxed. You'll be able to do more creative thinking at your own desk.

The Time Master Says
Classify the types of interruptions you receive, then you can cut them down and cope with them better.

Let's Play Concentration

I once heard anxiety defined as "the attempted unification of opposing forces." When you feel anxious, stop and determine which opposing forces you're attempting to unite. Are you working on a low-level task when something more important beckons? You feel anxious. Your intuitive alarm system is ringing.

Your anxiety stems from your attempt to work on a low-level project (force #1) when you know there's something else more appropriate for you to be working on (force #2).

Pause!
Be gentle with yourself. Give yourself more than a few days to focus more and multitask less.

One Thing at a Time

To become a master of doing one thing at a time, pick an activity you enjoy where you can engage in it without doing anything else, for example, driving your car with the radio off, reading in your favorite armchair without snacking, or listening to music instead of banishing it to the background.

➤ Start with small steps. If you're reading in your favorite armchair, promise yourself you'll go ten minutes without any snacks the first night, 15 minutes the second night, and so on. You might soon be reading for an hour without resorting to snacks.

➤ Find as quiet and comfortable a place as possible if you're involved in creative problem solving.

➤ If confronted by many tasks competing for your attention, identify the one that's most important to tackle, and stay with it until you're done (or for as long as you can stay with it).

➤ If you're temporarily pulled away from an important task by something else, return to the important task as soon as practical and stay with it to completion or for as long as you can.

Suppose it's your job to handle many items competing for your attention. If so, give short bursts of full attention to the task at hand, before turning to the next, and the next.

Observe an airline reservation attendant in a high pressure situation. The approach is one person-and-ticket at a time; often the attendant doesn't even look up from the computer monitor. The same principle holds for a good bank teller, a good bus driver, or a construction worker five stories above the ground.

Focus, Focus, Focus

Here are more tips to stay focused on the task at hand:

➤ Initiate personal balancing techniques: take deep breaths, stare out the window, visualize yourself tackling the situation easily.

➤ Close your eyes for a few seconds before confronting the task again.

➤ Use the J-4 interruption-management system cited earlier in this chapter.

➤ Observe the people in your organization who concentrate well. What do they do differently from everybody else? Talk to them; learn from them.

➤ If it's necessary, bring earplugs to work. Use a sound screen if it helps. (See Chapter 10, "Becoming A Snooze-Savvy Sleeper.")

➤ Let others in on your quest to increase your powers of concentration. Mutual reinforcement can help.

When Multitasking *Is* Permissible

For the most part, leave multitasking to computers. However, the few times when it's permissible to do more than one thing at a time usually occur away from work. Obviously, at dinner with a friend or loved one you talk and eat, but that can be seen as one event.

It's okay to drive and listen to the radio, or CDs. The exception is when the volume level impairs your concentration: you don't hear that ambulance.

Exercising with an iPod is iffy. At my health club, I was bemused to see a lady who was not only on the stair-climber with an iPod, but she then opened a book and started to read. I almost asked if she wanted some gum to chew.

Other activities where it's okay to double up include walking and talking with a friend, taking notes as you listen to a lecture, and talking to your lover while you're having sex (depending on your partner, this can enhance the experience).

CHAPTER 21

Treading Lightly—
And Loving It

In This Chapter:

➤ Streamlining your life leads to great things
➤ Taking stock of your priorities
➤ How to pare it all down a little each day
➤ Make your personal systems simpler

Chapter 21 is all about merging and purging: clearing out what you don't need so you can have more of a "life" each day.

Are you ready to tread lighter in this life? Merging and purging files (and other things you're hanging on to) is more than good housekeeping; it's essential because even with all our high-tech tools, paper will continue to mushroom for the foreseeable future. Once you let go of many of the items you're retaining, you'll experience a sense of freedom.

The Benefits of Paring Down

Contemplate all you encounter in the course of a day, week, month, and year: memos, reports, newspapers, bills, newsletters, bulletins, magazines, calendars, promotional items, and that's only the beginning. How would your life be if you regularly merged and purged these items as they came into your life?

You'd have more time because accumulations, by their nature, rob you of your time. First you acquire them, then handle them, look at them, move them, attempt to arrange them, file some, and discard others.

You're hanging onto too much stuff, and it's weighing you down. When are the best times to merge and purge what you've retained?

➤ When you approach a birthday, particularly a zero-year birthday. If you're about to hit 40, this is a great time to toss what you no longer need. Age 30, age 50, and age 60 work as well.

➤ Approaching New Year's is a good time.

➤ Spring-cleaning is a good time for clearing out the old and making room for the new.

➤ The arrival of fall (near summer's end, around Labor Day) works as well.

➤ Merge and purge when you move: no sense in paying movers to haul marginal "stuff" to your new location.

➤ When you change jobs or careers, you'll have to clean out your old desk at work.

➤ Passing one of life's milestones such as the birth of a child, the death of a parent, graduation, retirement, or earning a major raise can serve as reminders to re-examine what you're retaining. Rearrange your affairs to accommodate the new you.

➤ Any time the spirit moves you is a good time to merge and purge.

➤ As you finish reading this paragraph, put down the book and merge and purge in some area of your life. Make it an easy win, something you can tackle and master in ten to 15 minutes.

Merge and purge right after you've filed your taxes. After you've finished filing, benefits accrue. For one, you can chuck most receipts and documents from the tax year three years prior to the one you've completed. You have to hang on to the forms filed, but not the nitty-gritty details. (If you've been audited, or if you anticipate tax problems, that's a different story.)

Coming to Terms
Something that accrues builds over time.

Merging and Purging Mastery

When you don't feel in control of your time, everything in your life might seem as one big blur. The easiest way to approach merging and purging is to examine the important compartments of your life one at a time.

Examine your desk and what needs to be done there, then your entire office, where you live, your car, and other places in your life. Here are some suggestions:

➤ Maintain a file folder, notebook, or magazine box where you keep all travel-related materials. This might include booklets on hotels and destinations, passports, and vacation club folders.

➤ Merge and purge related to key service providers, records related to your automobile, insurance forms and policies, and other areas where efficiency matters. It takes a little time to merge and purge what you've retained and get it into a streamlined, highly useable form. Once you do, your efficiency level will soar.

➤ Around your office or workspace what can be consolidated, reduced, eliminated, relocated, or donated? Is the layout serving you well? Do you now need to move things to improve your daily efficiency? Can hard-copy items be scanned so that you no longer need the hard copy?

➤ At home, if you maintain a home office, apply all these methods and go a step further. For example, could you use a 31-day tickler file in your home as well as the one you use in your office?

What Can You Consolidate?

Can you consolidate family-related records so that you're in greater control? For example, all of Tommy's documents related to grade-school enrollment, immunization, early-school-dismissal policy, and summer camp could be kept in the same three-ring binder. All records related to your car (purchase documents, tax information, repair records, inspections passed, registration, and equipment installations) could fit into one file.

The Time Master Says
It's better to keep your car records in your home office. You can always keep a back-up of much of the documentation discussed here, buried someplace in your car's trunk.

Your car is an important area of your life and, based on what might have accumulated, requires merging and purging as well:

➤ Can you put all your credit cards, library cards, and the like into a secondary wallet to be hidden someplace in the car? I do this rather than carrying a wallet with 12 different cards in it because at any given moment, the only cards I actually need are my driver's license, one ATM card, and one credit card.

Anytime I might use one of the other cards, I'm usually with my car. By safely stashing the cards that I would only use with my car someplace within the car, I free myself from carrying all of them. This has several time-saving advantages. One, you're less likely to lose a majority of your cards if you lose your wallet. Two, it's easier to find your license, major credit card, and ATM card if they are the only ones you carry in your wallet.

As a safeguard you might want to copy all your credit cards and library cards on a copier, and keep a backup sheet at home and hidden in your car. (If cars disappear frequently in your neighborhood, skip this one!)

Use your glove compartment, any compartment between your two front

Pause!

If you're high on the prospect of stream-lining your life, then pare down a little at a time; you already have a full-time job and a raft of responsibilities.

seats, the trunk, or whatever space you have. Essentials such as car registration and proof of ownership stay snug at the bottom of my glove compartment.

Reflect and Win

To organize lots of little items use individual envelopes, small plastic sandwich bags, or clear Zip-lock baggies. This enables you to see what's inside and keeps the items dry and together.

Control Your Possessions and Your Time

Half the trouble of staying in control of your time is controlling your possessions. You have to keep tabs on so much that merging and purging could almost be a full-time job. Occasionally consume one Saturday morning putting these systems in place, and you'll find that the payoffs come back to you over and over again.

Don't attempt to tackle all arenas of your life on the same morning. You won't finish and the process itself might scare you away for a long time. To cut down a little at a time without breaking your stride:

➤ Anytime you're waiting for someone at work, at home, or in your car, use the extra few minutes to pare something where you are. If you have to drive your children around town a lot, after a few days you ought to have your car's glove compartment and trunk whipped into shape.

➤ When you've finished a big project at work and you're not ready to tackle some other major, intellectual pursuit at the moment, pare your holdings as a form of transition. For example, if you've finished a big report, can you delete previous versions? Can you chuck notes that are no longer needed?

Winning Back Your Time via Less Commuting

Traffic in most urban and suburban areas continues to become worse. There might be no meaningful solutions for decades. All the prognostications about people telecommuting and using video phones to conduct conferences with participants at remote locations haven't emerged to any significant degree.

In most metro areas, progression into the downtown centers is essentially a one-way flow at the beginning of the day and a one way flow out at the end of the day.

In my last job before becoming self-employed, I moved across the street from my office. I lived in a high-rise building, and my balcony was literally in sight of most of the peer group with whom I worked. However, no one actually figured out that my condo was at that location. So, even sitting out on the balcony at 5:00 or 6:00 p.m. for years never resulted in being spotted by a coworker.

All the while, however, I had a four-minute commute to the office, and that was on a bad day. Moving close to work is not an option for most people, but if it works for you, oh boy is that a fabulous time saver!

PART 6

Your Relationship, Your Time, and Your Peace of Mind

Part 6
Your Relationship, Your Time, and Your Peace of Mind

Wouldn't it be nice to apply much of what you've learned thus far to the personal aspects of your life? The chapters here focus on making time for each other—as in a partnership, having some kind of life when you're a parent, carving out real leisure in your life, considering taking a sabbatical, and keeping everything in perspective.

If you've been thinking, "It would be nice to have some kind of home life," you'll want to get started immediately. On the other hand, if your first thought is, "What's a home life?", you, too, are an excellent candidate for gaining great insights from the chapters that follow. Either way, you're hooked.

CHAPTER 22

The Couples Corner

Finding (or Making) Time for Each Other

In This Chapter:

➤ Connection and cooperation

➤ Exhaustion overrules vibrant relationships

➤ Men have needs, too

➤ Making your relationship Job One

This chapter focuses on how to carve out time for yourself and your partner which, for many people, is the supreme benefit of winning back your time.

At age 46, Jacquie is the new chief executive officer of a manufacturing company that produces home security devices. She believes that the best way to manage your time most efficiently is to stay completely focused on what you want to accomplish.

Her work responsibilities include heading four divisions, managing six affiliates, maximizing shareholder value, reporting to the board of directors, and keeping the operations profitable.

Is Life only Routine and Regimen?

CEO Jacquie begins her work day soon after arising, which is 6:15 sharp every morning. The night before she mapped out what she'll tackle in the morning. She spends the first three hours at home, then proceeds to the office for a 9:45 arrival. She departs from work when she feels satisfied with what she's accomplished usually between 7 p.m. and 10 p.m.

"I'm passionate about my work," she says, "and ruthless about how I allocate my time. If somebody wants to present a plan unaligned with my objectives, I don't devote a second to it. I steer them in another direction and don't give them any encouragement."

"I can't remember the last time I had a business lunch, they take too huge a chunk out of the middle of your day. Most times, I have a salad and a slice of pizza, or a bowl of soup right in my office. It is important to connect with others, so occasionally I schedule to meet people for a light dinner after work or, for light refreshment after that."

Jacquie has never been married and has no children. By the standards of most, she has no social life. She doesn't do errands, shop, or cook. There's practically no food in her kitchen, and if anybody ever dropped by, she'd have nothing to offer them.

Her routine, one that's become comfortable for her, maximizes her time. It wouldn't work for most of us. For us, other people, interests, and demands exist beyond our jobs.

It's relatively easy to manage your time if you live alone with no significant other to converse with, make plans with, or accommodate. You'll face your work and domestic challenges, but by comparison to those who have a meaningful relationship with someone else, managing one's time is less of an issue.

Connectedness Takes Work

Here, we'll address the dynamics of couples—married or not, with children or not—and discuss how they can carve out some time for each other. In the chapter that follows, we'll tackle the more involved notion of carving out time while maintaining effective parenting.

Focusing on the traditional man-wife couple, let's first consider common elements of the woman's perspective.

Couples who have a close relationship continually put energy and effort into it. Their union doesn't happen by chance, although some blessed individuals have personal chemistry that seems to jibe with one another to the nth degree. Even among those lucky couples however, a high degree of listening, cooperation, and respect for one another's schedules prevails.

Coming to Terms

The term nth degree means as far as possible, nearly limitless.

Women: Long Hours at Work and at Home

Women hold jobs outside the home in addition to maintaining the brunt of household responsibilities. Sociology professor Veronica Tichenor, from the University of Michigan, observes that women put in long hours at the office "because they enjoy it." Yet, they still do most of the housework because they want to or feel they have to. This includes even top female executives.

Part of the appeal of work are the indicators every step of the way, to let you know if you're on track, meeting the quota, and turning a profit. You receive evaluations, raises, performance appraisals, and promotions. What is the corollary at home? How do you know when you're a good partner, spouse, or lover?

Get a Wife (or the Equivalent)

Some working women conclude that they would have a wonderful life if they had the equivalent of their own "traditional wife" who stayed at home, kept the house in order, took care of the kids, cooked the meals, and handled all the errands. Today, this is an alternative for the ultra-rich; typically women do the housework, no matter how demanding or exhausting their work might be.

In studies, many women indicated to Tichenor that regardless of their achievements in the workplace, they still feel a strange and strong need to be regarded as excellent homemakers. If you're a woman, you probably already know and feel this on many levels. If you're a man, keep reading, because it's going to be the key to your carving out time for one another.

"A woman's responsibility for her family is a 24-hour task. Her time plan is a plan for living. There must be time allowance for the necessary work of the household, such as food preparation, serving, cleaning, and laundering. Family obligations, however, do not cease with the completion of the technical work of the home. There are children to be trained, supervised and enjoyed; the interests and activities of other adults in the family group must be shared; time for civic interests as well as for social activities and obligations must enter into the larger concept of time management for the housewife."—Irma Gross and Mary Lewis, Home Management (1938).

Many women fall into this syndrome, but as Irma Gross and Mary Lewis recounted in *Home Management*, ". . . the wise homemaker still will not let the interests listed above make such inroads upon her time as to unbalance her living in terms of health and personal development." They recommend "time for rest, sleep, recreation and hospitality, together with sufficient leisure to pursue some phase of living that will keep her emotionally stable and intellectually alert."

This 1938 book admonished its female readers that if their housekeeping was too disorganized, it could "interfere with the development of the various members of the family and their happiness of association."

From this—and a ton of other materials one could assemble from 1938, before, and even after—it's easy to see why women have an ingrained notion of having sole responsibility for the complete management of the household. While they appreciate any help others provide, regardless of what else is going on in their life, they often regard the state of their home as akin to the state of their being. (Guys, are you reading closely?)

Hired Help is a Big Help

Particularly among executive women, there's been movement towards maintaining outside services to help manage the household. When dollars permit, there's less reticence to bringing in a nanny, cleaning crew, gardener, window-washer, and delivery services. Women today buy prepared food for a dinner party, whereas in previous years they would not have.

Outside services? Yes, use them to the max! Where is it written that your guests will leave unsatisfied because your food was catered rather than personally prepared by you? Is it somehow unholy to pay someone to take care of a task you'd prefer not to do, and to free up hours for you so you could earn more per hour than the person you're paying?

Your Partner or the Rest of the World

In 1989, while writing the first edition of *Breathing Space: Living and Working at a Comfortable Pace in a Sped Up Society*, I noted that the crunch of too many things competing for one's time and attention was keeping couples apart from one another. Now, it's abundantly clear that this is so!

Reflect and Win

If you're in a committed relationship, every time you accomplish something through delegation—by relying upon the services and efforts of others—you potentially free yourself physically and emotionally to be more of a partner to your partner.

All the tasks, attention-diverters, and stimuli in your external environment, nearly guarantee that you'll have little left for your partner. You can be physically present, talk the talk and go through the motions, but to offer the complete essence of your being, means that you disengage from the mountains of minutia that over-complicate and glut the lives of most adults.

> **Pause!**
> When you're exhausted, do you want to be with anyone? Would you want to be with a partner who's exhausted? If you're both exhausted, will that benefit either of you?

Physically and Emotionally Drained

The highest divorce rates occur in the more complex, technically sophisticated societies. The nuances of fanning the flames of a relationship can't be given short shrift. If what's left of you after the over-information society has buffeted you for yet another day, how well will your relationship proceed?

The time that people spend on the Internet can be a contributing factor to their being apart from one another. For most of us, the majority of our online activity is done alone, at a desk or table, without anyone else present. If there is a loved one in the room, we are certainly not giving our full attention to that person.

An hour of earnest conversation between two people will always result in a higher level of connection, or at least understanding of one another, than simply sitting side by side and watching TV or some other screen.

The strongest relationships have a spiritual component that even transcends technology. People in such relationships can be away from each other for hours, days, weeks, months, and, in some cases, years and still maintain a strong connection.

Go Beyond Miniscule Efforts

Engaging in minuscule measures to free up some of your time and being, such as occasionally retaining outside help, is like rearranging deck chairs on the Titanic. If you feel the integrity of your relationship slowly starting to unravel—and if you value your relationship highly—to stay with the sea analogy, it's time to launch all ships.

➤ Delegate any task you possibly can.
➤ Let go of unrealistic standards that keep you mopping floors when you could be making love.
➤ Carve out a few minutes of uninterrupted time for each other every day—and several hours every weekend.
➤ Ask for help.
➤ Turn off the TV an hour earlier than usual, or don't turn it on to begin with.

➤ Schedule dates on your calendar.
➤ If both of your jobs allow for it, schedule unhurried lunches.
➤ Take short walks together after dinner.
➤ Leave nice notes around the house.
➤ Read a joke book together.

Males Are Here to Stay and Can Help Out

In many ways, the past few decades have witnessed considerable male-bashing. Males are seen as:

➤ Neanderthals
➤ Hot-blooded animals
➤ Uncouth detractors of society
➤ War-mongers
➤ Pumped-up athletes
➤ Exploiters of women
➤ Child-support deadbeats
➤ All of the above

In some circles, men are seen as disinterested in relationships, raising children, or staying for the long haul. Men have a good time and then they leave. If you find one you can trust, you're among the lucky few.

Beyond the obvious illogic, the banter above presupposes that an entire gender can be "wrong." From a bio-evolutionary and cosmic perspective, how can a gender be wrong? Men have needs, desires, and aspirations. A man in a relationship has needs, desires, and aspirations. And a man can be a domestic partner with his own set of chores.

Seeing Relationships in a Different Light

I counseled three couples as part of a feature story that ran on the front page of the *USA Today* lifestyle section. One of the couples was a minister and his wife. The wife lamented that with his growing congregation, she had less and less time to spend with him. Even Friday

Reflect and Win
Whether you've been in your primary relationship for 10 years or 10 weeks, an essential activity in making the relationship work and carving out time for each other is to look anew at your partner, to see what it would take to connect with and be with your partner on the highest level.

and Saturday evenings, which had been date nights for them, were now consumed by the minister's visits to sick or hospitalized congregation members.

Make it a Date Night

Most of the minister's visits lasted only 20 minutes, but by the time he got home, the magic of the evening was on the wane. I suggested a tactic to them that they felt was worth considering.

Hereafter, the wife would accompany her husband in the car on Friday and Saturday evenings whenever he called upon the sick. Because most of his visits lasted 20 minutes, she could sit in the car and read a magazine or listen to songs while he made his visit. When he was finished and returned to the car, they were each present, dressed, and ready to go. The night was still young and held great potential.

I caught up with her months after they put this plan into practice. It worked completely.

Creative Thinking Leads to Study Dates

By examining the responsibilities and activities of your partner, comparing calendars, and applying a dose of creative thinking, you might surprise yourself as to the amount and quality of time you can carve out for one another.

I had a girlfriend who was studying for the CPA exam. Her preferred method of studying was to go to a university library, with all her books and paraphernalia and a few snacks. She'd find a big table in the corner and camp out for hours. In the past, this was a lonely but necessary undertaking for her. Few of her previous boyfriends found this to be enticing. I thought this was pretty close to heaven. I was always working on new outlines for speeches and researching for books and articles.

Oh, what fun to be able to go to the library with someone who was equally intent on studying, while being together. We would work for 50 minutes and then take 10-minute breaks walking and talking. Then we'd get back to work and repeat the process. When it was done, we'd go out for pizza. I got much done during those sessions. She passed her CPA exam, on her first try!

Your Relationship: Job One

For a relationship to work in these harried times, it has to be the most important element in each partner's life. If the relationship comes in second to work, chances are that the vibrancy of the relationship will dwindle.

If you're a career-climbing overachiever, this doesn't mean you have to mute your goals or aspirations, or become someone you weren't intending to be. Plot your career strategy in the context of being in a committed relationship. This will work.

Successful people often have strong and committed relationships. It's no coincidence. They draw strength and sustenance from this relationship. Many report that it gives them a sense of freedom.

Coming to Terms

Sustenance is a source of nourishment, strength or support.

What are the hallmarks of a relationship where partners make time for each other without ignoring the other aspects of their lives? Foremost is respect for each other. During the early part of a relationship, when you're in rapture with one another, it's easy to show respect. You're on your best behavior.

Once the initial rush is past (or the honeymoon is over)—and for some people this can be 18–24 months or longer—many partners begin taking each other for granted. This is so even if one or both parties had sought the right relationship for years!

Here are some ideas on how respect is played out among couples who *intend to make time* for each other:

➤ When some time opens up for one partner, the other partner is immediately called to see about availability. The relationship continues to come first.

➤ They constantly ensure that they understand one another. They talk, debate, or argue until they've cleared up an issue. They don't broad-brush over differences, but work toward an understanding. The longer they are together as a couple, the more adept they become at this.

➤ They continually validate each other, tell each other what they appreciate about each other, find the good in each other, and emotionally support each other as often as practical.

➤ They acknowledge and recognize each other for the little things that each of them does. They also express their appreciation in vivid terms.

➤ They are reassuring to one another. They know that no partner comes without weaknesses, and while it's easy to love the facets about someone that please us, accepting the whole person is a challenging task.

Reflect and Win

At the close of the day some successful couples recap what the other did that was pleasing. "I appreciated your coming to the office to drop off the package." Or, "Thanks for cheering me up when nothing was working for me earlier today."

➤ They're devoted to one another. They don't allow other people to come between them.

➤ They convey a strong sense of caring. They leave notes to each other. They send messages, leave phone messages, and place small gifts in odd locations so that the partner encounters them when it's least expected.

➤ They recognize that no matter how busy they are with their careers and other activities, keeping the relationship alive takes work. Each is committed to devoting the time and energy to keep their relationship alive, and each partner knows it.

Pause!

Do you know others who profess to be in a committed relationship but give it short shrift? Take a look at yourself—if this description fits you, re-visit your priorities before your relationship is damaged.

Winning couples carve out time and attention for each other almost automatically as they proceed each day.

When the relationship is foremost in each of the partner's lives, time for each other materializes in ways that don't happen for other couples.

On the High Road to a Strong Relationship

If you're ready for action, here's a potpourri of strategies and techniques to help your relationship back on to the high road.

Paging All Baby-Sitters

Call everyone in the local community shopper newspaper who advertises baby-sitting services. Also post your own ads and develop a roster of eight to ten qualified, local baby-sitters so that you're *never* at a loss for one when you need one. Also enlist grandparents, relatives, and anyone nearby who could serve in the same capacity. Don't let your relationship and social life hinge upon your ability to find a baby-sitter on any given evening.

Pick a Mini-Date Night

Set aside one night per week as a mini-date night. This could be having a light workout together, cooking on the grill, strolling through a mall, playing Scrabble or cards, or anything else . . . other than watching television or a movie (too much focus on the screen and not on each other).

Kids Want Attention

If you have children—the topic of the next chapter—schedule to have time together while your kids are attending classes or activities. Plan to drop them off together, spend the first few minutes seeing what they're doing, then taking off for a walk or whatever, and returning to be with them for the last few minutes as well.

Marriage Groups to Encounter

Investigate local marriage encounter groups. These are usually weekend affairs where you're able to forge stronger marital bonds in a safe, relaxing, atmosphere that enables couples to talk quietly to each other about their lives and relationship.

> **Pause!**
> Don't knock marriage encounter groups until you've tried them. Couples who attend say that the experience has been rejuvenating for their relationship or marriage.

Little Things with Large Meaning

Therapists agree that having mom and dad depart for a weekend for time together is healthy for children. Kids need to know that their mom and dad can have fun together, without them.

If you can't or don't want to be away, take time off by walking around the lake, playing some favorite songs, having a picnic in the backyard, thumbing through your photo albums, or going to brunch at that four-star hotel.

> **Reflect and Win**
> Traditions between couples and within families are under-rated. By making the most out of recognizable dates on the calendar, you establish the potential to celebrate again and again.

Establish Non-holiday Family Traditions

Don't merely acknowledge birthdays, *celebrate* birthdays! Also, do something special for your anniversary, or the anniversary of the start of your relationship, of graduations, promotions, relocations, and special achievements in each of your lives. Mark these on both your calendars far in advance.

The Time Master Says

Make time for each other and celebrate all the special events that you can in your lives.

CHAPTER 23

Calling All Parents

In This Chapter:

➤ The family in flux
➤ Good parenting means sacrifice
➤ How fathers can pick up some slack
➤ Planning for family events

This chapter will help you to better manage your time with respect to raising kids.

Surveys conducted by leading pollsters show that adults feel as if children now are more spoiled than children of their own generations. They have more material objects, are more likely to be overweight and not physically fit, are less likely to participate in household chores, and might have worse manners. These are the same adults who have raised these kids and have the most influence over them in the formative years.

Movie producers market their PG-13- and R-rated films to attract 11 to 12-year-olds. Television commercials are increasingly zealous in their pursuit of the youth market, and televised events are even worse (think Miley Cyrus, "dancing" to *Blurred Lines*). Advertisers seem to be boldly venturing forward without shame. Still, parental influence is a strong and viable force when applied appropriately.

Time and Effort; Payoff Forever

It takes time to raise a child effectively, but the rewards are self-apparent. Devoting lots of time to your child during early years invariably yields results, particularly if your child grows up to be a fully functioning, balanced, happy, well-adjusted adult. Seating your child in front of the TV and having it serve as a quasi-babysitter, in the long run, can prove to be costly.

In the early 1900s, 80 percent of households included children. Today, less than 33 percent of households have children. Fewer adults today are involved in parenting than at any time in the past 100 years.

Coming to Terms
Quasi means outwardly, seemingly, or apparently.

Concurrently, more than 50 percent of all children will spend some time during their upbringing in a single-parent home. Among white Americans, one child out of three is raised by a single adult—and among African-American children, it's more than seven out ten.

Pause!
Parenting today is more challenging than in previous generations. Married or not, most mothers are now employed. Most families require two incomes to reach their desired standard of living, putting single-parent families in financial straits.

Divorce rates in America hover near 50 percent of all marriages, and the likelihood of divorce increases with each remarriage. With fewer adults involved in parenting often comes resistance to support services and programs designed to help children.

Let's look at tips for managing your time with your kids despite the daily obstacles you might face.

It's a Different World

If you're the parents of a newborn, for the first three years at least, you'll likely be sacrificing your time and body in devotion to your infant. Some couples create an arrangement where one keeps working outside the home, while one becomes the primary caregiver, usually the woman, but in a growing number of cases, also the man.

The key to effective parenting is raising your child in a wholesome, nurturing, reinforcing atmosphere. This affords you the greatest opportunity for raising a brighter, more alert, healthier child. Happily, the things that good parents have done traditionally to raise their children remain largely the same.

➤ Read to your child.
➤ Hug, cradle, and comfort your child (especially important).
➤ Nurture your child in every way, by talking, playing, or simply noticing what he or she is doing.

One of the heartening developments of parenthood in the last few decades is greater involvement by fathers in their children's lives. One St. Louis-based accountant commented, "It's wonderful to be able to see your own children grow up." Surveys indicate that fathers today value being fathers as much as anything else in their lives.

Focus on Your Children

To raise an insecure and unconfident child, stay preoccupied all the time whenever you're with your child. Alternatively, giving complete attention to your child enables your child to feel more confident and at ease when you're not around. He or she begins to learn that sometimes Mommy or Daddy has important things to do and can't offer any attention. But, when Mommy or Daddy does give them attention, it's complete and undivided.

Kids Learn Around the Clock

How are you when you're not playing with your kids, but doing something else that sends them messages. How about the way you serve dinner, for example?

➤ Do you start and stop?
➤ Do you talk on the phone?
➤ Do you go upstairs to do something?
➤ Do you pull clothes out of the laundry?

Pause!

Not giving your child your complete and undivided attention when you're together sends negative messages on several levels—such as you can't manage your own affairs, you'll never have enough time to completely be together, the child isn't important, your loyalties are divided, and "I have to work harder for Mommy or Daddy's attention."

The Messages that You Give Your Kids

Here's a probing question. Would you act like that in front of company? If not, then why do so in front of your kids? Increasingly, we transmit our predisposition toward busy-ness to our children. Thus, the message that you give your children is that there's so much to do in life that you can't keep up if you simply sit at the table with them. That, in turn, tells your children that such an existence will be theirs as well.

The Time Master Says
Dinner is one part of the day when you want to be sure to give your children undivided attention. Serve them, and then sit with them for the whole time. Talk to them. Give them a strong, clear message that the pace of society has little effect on your family's ability to have an engaging dinner with each other.

Beware of Taking on Too Much

Amy takes tae kwan do lessons, starts as striker on the soccer team, plays piano, and has a big part in the school play. Jason is on the tennis team, takes trombone lessons, serves as a traffic monitor at school, and sits on the student council.

It's not enough to be a kid anymore, do your homework, earn good grades, have some friends, and leave it at that. Too many children emulate their yuppie parents: they're occupied every moment of the day.

A quick, but not easy, way to carve out more time for your children as well as for yourself (because you're schlepping them all over town) is to help them decide which highly desirable, enjoyable, fun-filled activity they will not participate in for at least the current season. Is the quality of their life likely to diminish? If anything, it might improve.

Let us not demean the value of engaging in activities that one enjoys, that make one more effective as a

The Time Master Says
One study found that with children from birth to age 18, whether the mother works outside the home or not, the father's parenting responsibilities were nearly the same!

human being, and that serve others. A fine balance, however, exists between engaging in some activities and being over-booked!

Are you the soccer coach, the scout master, and the fund drive chair? Do you do more for your community than for your kids?

The Kids Can Pitch In

A growing number of parents, particularly women, find that effective parenting today hinges on having kids pitch in with chores. At the least, kids need to be responsible for keeping their own room orderly. From about age six on, this needs to be an everyday habit. Until then, you'll probably have to help them.

From the time my daughter was three until 18, we practiced what I call the replacement principle. In a nutshell, whatever you add to the room merits one other thing being removed. Add a DVD? Sure. Which one do you want give up?

Kids and Their Homework Habits

Many kids don't receive adequate parental support concerning homework. If both parents work, they might be too tired to help or offer too much help, doing most of the homework themselves.

Your role as parent? To encourage your child to do his or her own homework in a timely manner as it's assigned and help out when needed, but not to do the homework.

The Time Master Says
As a rough guideline, about 15 to 20 minutes of homework per day is appropriate for children up to grade 2, about 30 to 60 minutes a day for grades 3 to 6, and up to two hours for middle school. In high school, assignments can vary widely, but beyond three hours daily might tax even the most ambitious students.

Studies invariably show that American kids do less homework than their counterparts in other countries, while watching more television and spending more time online.

In helping your children with their homework, here are guidelines:

➤ Set a regular time for homework every day.

➤ Establish ground rules as to what takes place during this time, with no electronic or entertainment-based intrusions.

➤ Set aside a desk or table so that your children will have a regular place in which to do homework.

➤ Assemble appropriate supplies such as pens and pencils, rulers, crayons, scissors, and pads.

➤ Be available to offer helpful suggestions and guidance only.

➤ Provide clues so that your child proceeds down the right path without actually receiving the answer.

➤ Offer lavish praise when a child has completed a difficult math problem or has written a nifty book report.

Reflect and Win

Behavior that's rewarded is repeated. If you want your children to do homework and to do it well, reward them for the good behavior that they exhibit, directly after they exhibit it such as praising them..

A Strong Connection with Your Kids

Homework or not, raising happy, well-rounded kids requires effective communication, much like a rewarding marriage or primary relationship. One survey, among parents of students ages ten–14, revealed that:

➤ Nearly half of all kids and one quarter of parents report that they spend less than 30 minutes daily in conversation with each other.

➤ Parents believe the top priorities for their children are having fun, being with their friends, and looking good. Children report that their top priorities are their future, their school work, and family matters. Thus many parents underestimate their child's maturity level and misconceive what's important to them.

➤ One in five kids indicates that it's easy to speak with their parents about issues that matter; one in four says it's difficult to talk about such things, and the rest report that it is "somewhat easy" to talk about such things.

Stay in Touch, or Lose Touch

Given the above, how do you reasonably stay in touch and convey to your kids that you care? Among many options, try these:

➤ Convey trust at an early age. If your children know that you listen to them, they'll open up to you about everything in their life, even about school, drugs, or sex.

➤ Your children, like anyone else, will feel pleased if asked for their opinions on issues big or little, it doesn't matter.

➤ Let them have their say. Don't anticipate what someone is going to say, or finish their sentences for them. You wouldn't do this at work, so don't do it with your children. Give them sufficient time to explain themselves; more time than you would afford to an adult.

➤ While you're letting them explain, pay attention to their body language and emotions. Are they holding back? Is there something they'd like to say but are not saying it well? Is there something they want you to draw out of them?

Reflect and Win

Listening can be ad hoc. Often, your child will open up to you while you're walking along, driving the car, or doing yard work. As you develop a bond and rapport with your child, opening up to one another could be spontaneous.

Get Coordinated for the Whole Week

Coordination is vital whether a mother and father, a mother alone, or a father alone take major responsibility for rearing and directing the affairs of their children. One mother of three comments that she always reviews her week in advance on Sunday evening, even if it's only for five to ten minutes.

If you arise each day and seek to determine what will get you and your children through the day, you're going to run into snags because your time horizon isn't broad enough. A peek at the whole week affords you a better opportunity to manage the pace with grace and encounter fewer surprises, fewer time crunches, and less anxiety.

Some family counselors believe that multi-week, month-long, or multi-month planning is desirable. As you plot the dates of birthdays, other family celebrations, time off from school, kid's lessons, and other events, you gain a broad picture of who needs to be where, when, and supplied with what.

Pause!

Is this too much? One parent prefers to plan as much as two years in advance. He frequently asks his children's teachers and school administrators the dates of events so that he can plot them on his calendar and ensure his participation. He sometimes has to force the dates out of others: they haven't planned their activities that far in advance!

The Value of Overestimating the Time Needed

The more accomplished, effective, and intelligent you are, the more likely you are to fall into a time trap. Your optimism combined with resourcefulness leads you to believe that certain tasks will take x amount of time. If it turns out they take 1.2 or 1.3 times your estimate, you're frustrated. Yet things rarely seem to be completed based on your own perceptions of how much time is required.

Overestimate the time that task or activity will take, especially in relation to your children. If you finish on time or sooner, you'll feel less frustrated.

Pause!

"People sometimes feel that everyone else is accomplishing more than they are, but that is usually because they overestimate what others do and underestimate what they themselves do," says Windy Dryden, professor of psychotherapeutic studies at Goldsmiths, University of London.

If you've over-scheduled your child and underestimated the time both of you will expend on activities (the least of which is chauffeuring!), you'll be perpetually frustrated. If you and, by extension, your child have the wherewithal to schedule less and be generous in your scheduling, you're apt to lead more serene, less hectic lives. You'll have a greater chance of enjoying the few activities you choose.

Caring and Sharing between Two Parents

If you're fortunate to be in a true parenting partnership with your spouse, both you and your children stand to benefit. Absent of hard-and-fast rules as to what equal parenting care givers are supposed to do, here are some ideas:

➤ Alternate who rises first on selected mornings to take care of breakfast and help the kids get dressed and ready for school.

➤ Alternate who rises first on the weekend.

➤ Divvy up household chores according to personal preference or inclination or, to remain completely egalitarian, based on a rotating schedule.

➤ Alternate who reads or plays with the kids. Alternate who chauffeurs the kids. Schedule who baby-sits, when the other parent needs some time away.

➤ Maintain equal contact and address information, including doctors, dentist, coaches, and teachers.

➤ Log in equal hours for emergencies, when the children are sick, or when one of the parents needs to break out of work.

Pause!

The mother's acceptance or lack thereof, of a potentially care-giving father, generally plays a dramatic part in whether or not the father is successful. Some mothers claim they are desirous of having the father play a more prominent role in raising the children, but these mothers don't understand the power that they have to make this happen.

Taking Stock: Where Are You Now?

If you examine your household calendar and it appears to be filled to the brim with kids' activities, consider how many of those activities you actually initiated, how many you participate in, and how many you enjoy. Don't be a martyr or a perpetually sacrificing parent.

Find a Buddy Onsite

Suppose your child plays in a little league. When you attend such functions, perhaps you meet and befriend another parent. Sitting in the stands, you both watch the games and have enjoyable conversations. It's one way to maintain a friendship, be a parent, and have a life.

Doubling Up: The Exceptions

I'm not a big fan of doubling up on activities, still, in some instances you can take your child to an event and at the same time can read or take care of some light paperwork.

In Durham, North Carolina, my daughter wanted to go to a play center called Amaze-N-Castles, all the time. We averaged about one visit per quarter.

During those visits, she darted into the maze, where she ran, jumped, climbed, swung, slid down tubes, threw balls, and exercised in every way. The 90 minutes or so that she played, I sat at a table and handled paperwork.

I'd look up every time she called out, and periodically monitored what she was doing when she didn't call. Meanwhile, for 90 percent of the time I was able to take care of my tasks. I was completely present in both the drive up and drive back, in helping her get started, and in playing together in the arcade section of the facility. Undoubtedly, you have corollaries in your life.

Stage a Mini-Workout

My daughter often preferred activities that didn't interest me, such as attending the gymnastics meets at the University of North Carolina. There were four events at these meets, including the balance beam, vaulting, the uneven parallel bars, and the floor exercise. The events were held in an 8,000-seat gym—and 7,600 of the seats were open—we could sit where ever we choose.

She watched intently. I watched as well and at the same time stretched and did light calisthenics and isometrics.

Reflect and Win

If your child clamors to watch DVDs, choose those that *you* would enjoy watching as well. Enough G-rated and PG-rated movies are available in which you both could find interest, especially in historical biographies, animal stories, intelligent animations, comedies, period pieces, and sci-fi.

As Your Child Learns . . .

It's rewarding to rediscover parts of your own childhood. My daughter Valerie tried skating once and was thrilled by it. She decided it was worth pursuing and wanted to take lessons. When her mother brought her to skating lessons, her mother decided to rediscover skating for herself and took private lessons while Valerie was in a group lesson elsewhere on the ice. So, it was double payoff.

CHAPTER 24

 # An Eye on Leisure

Are you short-changing your leisure? If so, Chapter 24 will help to put you back on the right track.

"Leisure" as a concept has been on the rocks since personal computers became popular. In our "24/7" society (and I loath both that term and the concept), shouldn't opportunities for leisure be more plentiful? After all, if everything is open all the time, then an array of options awaits you. Actually, the opposite is true. Knowing something is open and available all the time doesn't necessarily prompt you to take advantage of the extended hours.

When the Boundary Between Work and Leisure Blurs

Most people have an odd relationship with leisure—Americans, in particular. Numerous times in the previous century, we have struggled with this strange and frightening concept of leisure time; in fact, "it's not a place we're really comfortable with," noted Benjamin Hunnicutt, a professor of leisure studies at the University of Iowa. Hunnicutt exalts the value of having sufficient leisure in your life.

To define leisure as time away from work is to misunderstand the concept. One group of researchers defined it as that which is worth your time and attention, given that you otherwise face a minimum of limitations and/or responsibilities. It sounds a little clinical, but what it means is *a rewarding activity, free from work and preoccupation with work.*

Executives and entrepreneurs in industrialized societies attempt to accomplish more in the same amount of time by engaging in activities at a fast pace, doubling up on activities or giving less focused attention to activities. What's more, they often attempt to schedule any leisure activities in mind with greater precision. Alas, this approach does not lead to the experience of true leisure—rest, relaxation, regeneration, and renewal. Rather, it makes leisure much like everything else—scheduled too tightly, moving too quickly, involving many stimuli, and ending too soon.

Forced-Fit Leisure Feels Phony

When the boundaries between work and personal time blur, the perception is that you have no leisure at all. As I wrote in *Breathing Space*, if you attempt to force-fit leisure between periods of otherwise frenzied activity, your leisure will suffer.

Most people cannot start and stop on a dime—they can't be working hard one minute, and the next moment be totally engaged in some relaxing, rewarding activity. Human nature being what it is, we all tend to need some transition time.

Here is a small sampling of what people often miss because they don't "have time":

➤ Coming together for dinner as a family
➤ Making homemade dinners or baking bread
➤ Baking traditional holiday cookies
➤ Making gifts (and handmade valentines)
➤ Spending holidays together
➤ Sitting around with the family when it's not a holiday
➤ Relaxing and feeling at ease during family reunions

The Time Master Says
More than half of people polled regard leisure as "important" which makes one wonder about the well-being of those who regard it as not important.

➤ Going on excursions together
➤ Praying together (maintaining one's spiritual life)
➤ Taking a leisurely Sunday drive
➤ Attending cultural events (the opera or an art gallery)
➤ Dressing differently for different occasions
➤ Letting children be children (such as playing ball and not being rushed from one experience or activity to another)
➤ Putting children to bed with storybooks
➤ Reading religious books with your children
➤ Learning mother's recipes
➤ Learning to play a musical instrument
➤ Sewing one's own clothes
➤ Writing letters
➤ Planting a garden, then eating or canning the produce
➤ Exercising or taking leisurely, relaxing strolls
➤ Relaxing at a spa
➤ Reading a literary novel or epic
➤ Maintaining etiquette
➤ Courting (hookups don't count)

Transitions Can Be Crucial

When the U.S. troops began returning from World War II, they were assembled in large numbers, consigned to ships, and over many weeks or months slowly sailed home. The time on board enabled them to reflect with one another, decompress, and mentally and emotionally prepare themselves for reintegration into civilian society.

When they returned, many were greeted by celebrations or parades. Not everyone had a smooth transition, but the chance of reintegrating into a peacetime existence was heightened because of the nature and duration of the transition time.

Conversely, U.S. troops departing from the Vietnam War came home one at a time, via jet planes that transported them in less than 24 hours from a hellish environment back to the world they had left. Little or no transition time, no camaraderie with people who had shared a similar experience, and no time to mentally and emotionally prepare for re-entry into the civilian world, posed many challenges.

Most troops were not greeted as heroes or given celebrations.

Consequently, Vietnam-era veterans had the most difficult time reintegrating into society of any class of American veterans.

You Need Slack, Jack

You're not returning from war, but the principle remains. When you build leeway into your schedule, you gain psychic satisfaction that isn't otherwise generated. As you learn to know yourself better and better, you recognize that allowing ample time allocations for certain tasks is not going to turn you into a laggard.

Coming to Terms

A laggard, like it sounds, is a person who falls behind, trail others, or achieves little progress.

Sufficient leisure enables you to be as efficient as before while feeling less frustrated, more content, more energized, and ready for what's next.

Personally, building slack into my schedule is as critical as anything. Having some time when nothing is scheduled, whole days where it's not critical for me to do anything, is essential for my overall health and well-being. It helps me renew myself so that when I return to more vigorous pursuits, I have more internal resources at my command.

A Pleasant Commute

Another bit of history: following World War II, through the 1950s, as U.S. suburbs sprung up, and during much of the 1960s, the commute at the end of the day provided the mental and emotional transition time vital to enjoying one's time at home. The roads weren't so crowded. Seats were available on busses, trains, and subways.

Pause!

Building slack into your schedule allows you to stay in touch with your own natural timing.

Years passed, and commuting became a chore, then highly burdensome, then stressful—and now, for some, a prompt for outbreaks of rage and violence.

Today the commute for most people does not serve as a valid transition time between work and leisure. For many, it represents a daily ordeal. See Chapter 7 on priorities, "What Matters Most to You?" for commuting tips.

Suppose you're stuck in a daily arduous commute. You hate it—every morning you crawl along at a snail's pace down an interstate highway. However long it takes you to arrive, you perceive that it's three times as long. How do you turn such an ordeal into more productive time, where you're prepared to actually have a life the rest of the day?

Reflect and Win

In his book, *Your Body Doesn't Lie*, Dr. John Diamond revealed how classical music offers the right syncopation to help your body back into a more natural alignment. If you don't like classical music, play something else that's relaxing for you.

Condition your car: Use the time to check your air-conditioner, close all the windows, then play a CD or audio that you enjoy.

Make the interior of that car or, if you use mass transit, the personal space around you as supportive as you can. For some that means simply closing your eyes, donning earphones connected to an iPod, reading, or staring out the window.

Non-Speed Zone Ahead

Build in pockets of leisure periodically throughout the day and week to keep yourself in balance. For example, if you have a flight scheduled weeks or months in advance, mark on your schedule that the plane will be departing 30 minutes before it actually will.

What happens when it's time to take your flight? When you arrive at the gate, you realize that you have extra time: time to collect yourself, arrange your luggage, drink from the water fountain, go to the bathroom, center yourself, and feel good about what you're doing. Such opportunities are nearly always available—it's merely a matter of how you handle your affairs and prepare your schedule.

Side bar

To handle challenging tasks under tight deadlines, sometimes you need to slow down for a moment or two to be back in sync with your own nature, rhythm, and way of being. Hence, leisure gives you the ability to speed up when you need to.

Side bar

Boost Your Fun Potential

The notion of preparing for leisure might seem foreign to you at first, but it makes sense.

The last time you took a big vacation, you marked it down on your calendar, and perhaps reserved airline tickets or hotel accommodations. Undoubtedly you discussed the event with others in your family or with friends. You made plans, wrote notes, and spent money, all in preparation for this time away. Mentally and emotionally you geared yourself to the reality that it was coming. The same process is advantageous when it comes to experiencing leisure on a daily basis.

If you're committed to having more leisure in your life, be vigilant in your initial efforts. It takes guts to buck the norm in a society of frenzied, exhausted over-achievers.

It's too easy when immersed in such an environment to believe perpetual exhaustion is normal and acceptable. This is the underpinning of Dr. Erich Fromm's work.

A noted psychologist and author, Fromm made the observation decades ago that you might not be crazy after all, it might just be society. These days, he seems right on the mark.

Here, then, is your mini-plan to reserve time for leisure: leisure that you want, need, and deserve.

Mark it on the Calendar and Make it Arrive

When you plan for a big vacation, you add it to your schedule and undertake supporting behaviors to ensure that you depart as scheduled. Extend such behavior to lower-level leisure—the week-to-week and daily breaks that you want and need. Put low-level leisure time on your calendar:

➤ Look forward to it.
➤ Dwell on it.
➤ Talk about it.
➤ Make plans around it.
➤ Revel in it.

Treat leisure as an important component of your health and welfare and you won't have to be as vigilant about it in the future. For now, make a commotion about it.

Immerse Yourself, Leisure Counts

Treat leisure activities with the same reverence that you presently exhibit with key prospect appointments or, heck, trips to the tax auditor's office. Granted, occasionally compelling reasons arise as to why you need to change your schedule.

When it's time for the leisure activity to commence, be there, experience it, and immerse yourself. Allow the activity to be as important as any other. Let go of your left brain, eyes-on the-clock, my-career-is-everything predisposition. If you're shooting baskets, shoot baskets. If you're hiking, hike. If you're meeting with the garden club, meet with the garden club.

If you find yourself wishing to be elsewhere or seeking to do other things during the leisure time you've scheduled, change your leisure activity; perhaps you've picked the wrong one. However, don't shortchange how much time you devote to leisure.

Be Gone Guilt

Some people feel guilty when they work long hours because they feel that they should be with their kids, their friends, or elsewhere. Conversely, they feel anxious when they're with their kids, friends, or someplace else: they feel guilty for not working more.

When they take a vacation, they're overly concerned with what's going on back at the office. When they take a walk, they're concerned about the voice mail and emails that might have arrived while they were out of the loop.

Precious reader, you will *never* experience leisure and its benefits if you feel anxious about what else you could or should be doing or what you're missing.

Making Friends at Every Age

It's unfortunate, particularly for men, that as they age they tend to have fewer good friends in life. Women seem to make time for close and new friends at all ages. For sure, maintaining and cultivating friendships requires work and effort. The investment pays big dividends, however, because friendships enrich life.

Friends give you a support system beyond your family. They take you to new places or share insights new to you. Having good friends can even strengthen your marriage. If you're counting on your spouse to serve as the be-all and end-all, you're likely to be disappointed. Besides, depending on your interests, it might make more sense to go to the ball game or the opera with a friend rather than with your spouse.

Reflect and Win

Long-distance friendships can be hard to sustain, but creativity can keep them going. Whenever you're traveling for work, see if it's possible to create circular routes that include areas where your friends reside. Perhaps on your way back, you can stop off and see a good friend. If they're close by, all the better.

How can you easily keep up with your friends, i.e., ensure that they're in your path?

➤ Seek events where you can include your friends although you normally wouldn't think of it.
➤ Plan vacations at the same time and destination.

➤   Be members of the same local group, cause, or activity.

➤   Have a designated encounter each month, such as the last Friday.

➤   Introduce your spouses so they will get to know each other better, therefore increasing the probability of you seeing your friend more often.

Working to keep up these friendships will pay off in the long run with years of companionship. Is that worth a little of your time?

Getting Creative about Leisure

If you're single, your options for enjoying sufficient leisure abound. Depending on your work situation, you can depart at a moment's notice. You can take advantage of holiday weekends or perhaps go explore the possibility of going on sabbatical (the topic of the next chapter). If you're married—and perhaps with children—having leisure for yourself and having leisure for your family can be more of a challenge.

The trend in recent years has been toward more frequent but shorter vacations, often boxed around holiday weekends. If you take a contrarian approach and have your time off when the rest of the world isn't, then holiday weekends are a good time to stay at home and let everybody else compete for highway lanes and parking spaces.

In my book *The Smart Guide to Accomplishing Your Goals*, I list a wide variety of possible goals in various categories such as social, leisure, and lifetime goals. Here are some ideas on how to make the most of your leisure:

➤   Receive only magazines that make your life simpler or that amuse you.

➤   Take only non-stop airplane trips on vacation. Anything else taxes you in ways you don't need to be taxed.

➤   Buy bubble bath, even if you're unsure when you'll use it.

➤   Install a hammock in your backyard.

➤   Find new friends whose leisure activities are alluring and who will teach, guide, train, and include you in their activities.

➤   Open your home to others via parties, receptions, meetings, and brief visits.

➤   Find others in your town who like to play in ways that you like to play.

➤   Frequently take walks in shopping malls, along city sidewalks, down nature trails, and anywhere else that you feel safe.

➤   Visit the library one evening a week, and read whatever magazines appeal to you.

➤   Join a monthly book review discussion group.

➤   Buy a joke book, learn some card tricks, practice impersonating others, or learn juggling.

➤   Go on an impromptu weekend trip to someplace you haven't visited.

➤ Consider taking up a sport you've never attempted, such as golf, archery, hiking, or snorkeling. Or take a class on crafts, be it wood, pottery, metals, ceramics, leather, stained glass, jewelry, or woodworking.

➤ Become an amateur geologist, going on your own "fossil" hunts. This could be as simple as finding rocks and breaking them open, or looking for petrified shark's teeth, troglodytes, or minerals embedded in stone.

➤ Buy a telescope and start watching the sky.

➤ Train a hamster, a gerbil, a cat, or a dog.

➤ Volunteer for a committee that sponsors a festival, holiday parade, street fair, or exposition.

➤ Enroll in a course in handwriting, calligraphy, or sketching.

➤ Visit one new restaurant a month or, if the spirit moves you, once a week!

With your spouse or significant other, go to a restaurant much earlier than usual some evening, linger over drinks, linger over appetizers, linger over the entree, linger over dessert, and take your sweet time leaving as well. By the time you leave, the world will have changed. So will your attitude.

CHAPTER 25

Sabbaticals
Why You Might Want to Take One

If every cell in your body rebels at the notion of taking a sabbatical—"Where could I ever find the time?" or "Who can afford it?"—then all the more reason for you to peruse this chapter.

A Time and a Purpose for Everything

The universe is governed by laws. Some laws are readily apparent, such as laws of cause and effect, laws of gravity, and the laws of motion. Somewhere in the big book of karmic order, it says that ever so rarely you need major time off. Forget all the logical explanations as to why this is all but impossible, and stay with me.

Earlier chapters have discussed the likelihood of your living and working longer. The longer you work, the greater the odds are that you need time away from work. If the need for income, to watch over Michael and Michelle, or simply to feed Rover were not issues, could you mentally and emotionally acknowledge that your inner and outer beings desperately crave a month or three months away from work?

Upon returning from 90 days in the Andes Mountains in South America, one man from Sacramento remarked that as he started his sojourn, it took 15 days before he actually realized how long he was going to be away. His sabbatical included no TV, no email, and no

Reflect and Win

Taking a sabbatical from work is not for everyone nor practical for many people, although everyone could probably benefit. Even if you can't foresee the possibility now, a sabbatical might be in your future.

cell phone. He did phone home every couple days to ensure that the place was still standing. Otherwise, this was to be a time of deep reflection, renewal, and restoration of the parts of him that he feared were all but lost.

Faculty members at colleges and universities have long been privy to the benefits of taking a semester-long sabbatical, with pay, every six to seven years. With a little planning and forethought, many university professionals extend their sabbaticals by taking a second semester off, usually without pay, hence racking up eight–12 months away from the ivory tower.

Coming to Terms

Restoration, in the personal sense, is a conversion or return of something that was missing.

Programs Vary Widely

Corporate sabbaticals, the kind in which you're much more likely to be interested, vary widely. Most tend to be short. Three months would be a long time; two months or one month is the norm. They're also likely to be unpaid.

Sabbatical programs in companies make for interesting reading. For example, one high tech company allows its vice presidents to award high-achieving employees up to eight weeks of paid vacation. Employees with seven years tenure who are consistently high performers are eligible. One award winner spent his time learning about astronomy, and hand drawing. He also took his father on a golfing trip.

Another firm offers a three-week paid sabbatical to employees after five years of tenure. This bonus is added to the employee's annual personal days of vacation. The departing employee has to give his or her manager 60 days notice.

One law firm grants its partners a six-month *paid* sabbatical after five years as a partner, and again every six to seven years thereafter. So far, all partners taking sabbaticals have returned—no one has taken a sabbatical, and then changed firms, changed professions, or, for that matter, retired.

For non-partners, three months with pay are granted after ten years of service and then every seven years thereafter.

➤   Another law firm offers its partners three months of paid time off every eight years.
➤   An investment banking group has no formal sabbatical program but employees are granted leave on a case-by-case basis.
➤   A mutual fund tracking firm offers a six-week paid sabbatical every four years for all employees.

Some Compelling Reasons Companies Offer Sabbaticals

Why would a company offer sabbaticals at all? Isn't it a hardship when key employees leave for months at a time? What if they are members of a team (which is likely)? The driving notion is that the sabbatical regenerates and renews employees and is a viable antidote against burnout.

Competition for talented employees in some industries is vigorous, and companies will do what they can to retain the best. So sabbaticals are provided as a recruiting tool to attract top talent or as a reward to keep valued employees.

Companies might employ sabbaticals as a way to bolster their downsizing plans. A public relations manager for a telecommunication firm commented that the company expects that a percentage of those on sabbatical will not return, and so that "diminishes the need to downsize."

Many companies believe that sabbaticals offer key employees a way to learn, grow, and ultimately be more valuable to the firm. Indeed, the probability of most people bettering themselves and bringing new skills and perspectives back to the workplace has proven to be a bonanza.

> **The Time Master Says**
> Some companies offer paid sabbaticals with the provision that the time off be used for some specific purpose, such as community service, learning, or travel.

The Time Masters Says

Sabbaticals are an international phenomenon. In the United Kingdom, the number of organizations offering sabbaticals increased over the span of a decade.

Endless Options When it Comes to Sabbaticals

Often, companies grant sabbaticals to employees who will be engaged in job-related study or research. A lesser number of companies grant them for employees simply seeking rest or vacation, and a slightly lesser number for non-job related study.

Some firms maintain a policy of one week's extra leave for each year of service. So, if you've been working for someone for six years, you're entitled to a six-week sabbatical.

More organizations realize that as the nature of work intensifies, and as the number of hours logged in by management staff increases, taking a break beyond annual vacation time benefits both employer and employee.

One worker returning from a sabbatical said that he hadn't taken a break during his professional career. When he returned to work he had more confidence and energy, hence benefitting his company. Being away was refreshing and rejuvenating. "The sabbatical gave me a chance to take stock, put things in perspective, and be clearer about what I wanted out of life," he says.

If you're a techie, your odds of taking a sabbatical are decent. Silicon Valley companies who compete fiercely for top talent, and where many employees devote their minds and bodies to the job effort, often use sabbaticals as part of their bait.

A bio-technology company offers full-time employees a sabbatical of six continuous weeks with full pay and benefits beyond their annual vacation time, starting in their seventh year of employment. The head of human resources at the company observed that the sabbatical program was one of many rewards offered to employees for superior performance. In essence, in exchange for a high level of commitment, the company bestows the incentive of a more significant break than is typically offered.

Pause!

Many experts agree that sabbaticals work best if not regarded merely as time off to recover from a variety of stress-related maladies.

One of the biggest benefits of a sabbatical is the basic acknowledgment that you're going to experience a long time away from the job. That, in itself, can result in favorable physiological and psychological benefits. If you know that six months from now you'll have three months off, you can plan your affairs accordingly and perhaps pace yourself for the six months as well.

You want to approach your time off on an even keel. Remember, the sabbatical is not designed to overcome high stress, job-related maladies. Such challenges need to be taken care of while on the job.

Eliminating the Obstacles to Departing

On your way to realizing that you, too, can take a sabbatical, you might need to overcome some mental obstacles. The common ones are *having enough money, caring for kids,* and *making a smooth transition back.* Let's mow 'em down in order.

Reflect and Win

Some employers fear having employees go on sabbaticals because they believe employees will use that time to look for new jobs. Data doesn't bear this out. Also, if you and your employer discuss what you'll be doing when you return, you increase the probability of a smooth re-connection.

Money Concerns?

The more time you have before a sabbatical, the more time you have to plan your finances accordingly. Your daily expenses when not working are usually less than when working. You don't have the commuting, corporate lunch, dry-cleaning, and variety of other expenses that add up in the course of a month.

You can wear more comfortable clothing—and wear it more often—eat less expensively (and maybe eat more healthfully), and forego expenditures related to keeping up with the corporate Joneses. You can walk and bike instead of taking a car.

If you opt to travel during your sabbatical, you can find low-cost lodging all over the world. You can also join a vacation club or home-swapping programs, and essentially pay nothing for long-distance lodging.

If you're going on a paid sabbatical, then you have even fewer monetary concerns.

What to Do with the Kids?

If you have young children, and you're their primary care provider, chances are you can't take a sabbatical. Or, maybe, you can bring them along.

If your children are a little older, perhaps there's a neighbor, relative, grandparent, or semi-willing spouse who'll grant you a month or two months to depart. Perhaps they'll do it in exchange for you doing the same for them some time. Maybe they'll do it for you out of the goodness of their hearts.

If you have no children, you have no excuse.

The Time Master Says

While it might be emotionally difficult to spend one month away from your children, it could be an enriching experience for everyone. You can stay in touch by phone and e-mail. Your children will gain a different perspective on life without you around for the time you're taking off. They might appreciate, respect, and love you more upon your return— a triple bonus.

Will I Fall Behind My Colleagues?

Could a couple months away put you behind when you step back into the office? In today's over-information society, no one has a long-term lock on what's coming down the pike. In many respects, the two months or so that you're away will be an advantage because of the newfound perspectives that you'll gain.

You can quickly catch up on the corporate memos and scuttlebutt. That'll take maybe half a day. A co-worker can bring you up to speed on any new programs or procedures in a couple hours here and there, and such learning might be more productive than learning on your own, had you been there all along.

Within one week of your being back, you might feel as if you haven't missed out on anything. You're more likely to feel as if your time away was too brief, like a distant dream.

An Action Plan to Get Started

Here's a brief action plan to help you make leaving a reality. Review Chapter 1, "The Overtime Epidemic: How to Nip It In the Bud," where you learned the vital steps for ending work at a reasonable time at least one day per week, and then escalating it to more than one day. Much of the same philosophy applies here.

Make It So: Allow That It Can Happen

Adopt the notion that it can be done; you can take a month or two or longer away from work. Having done that, now pick the actual time because someday never comes. If you keep postponing the time when you'll take a sabbatical, the chances are it will never happen. One obligation after another will creep up, and any windows of opportunity will close right up.

It pays to visit internet sites that offer insights and reflections on sabbaticals.

Pause!

The likelihood of you taking a sabbatical is directly related to your ability to set a firm departure date, save a tidy sum (if it's a non-paid sabbatical), and announce to all that it's going to happen. Otherwise, it's not going to happen.

"I'm Going to Do It!"

Once you're firmly committed, here are the steps to make it so:

1. When you've picked the date, mark it on your calendar. Then circulate a message to co-workers, staff, peers, and anyone else. Break the news to your family as well, if applicable.
2. Set up a savings plan with your employer, bank, or other financial institution so that a specific (and sufficient) amount will be extracted from your paycheck each week, in anticipation of building to a sum that will see you through.
3. Secure with your employer that all benefits still accrue.
4. Talk with your boss about the plans he or she has for you upon your return. Build in some slack time so that you can re-acclimate without feeling overwhelmed when you return. Print an actual memo in writing as to what your tasks and responsibilities will be that first week, for the second week, and thereafter. Then securely file it.
5. Send a reminder message about your time away to all correspondents, as the magic time approaches,.
6. Arrange with staff support, your family, and all others how you want messages to be fielded, mail to be allocated, and other correspondence to be handled in case you will not be directly privy to these communiques on your sabbatical.
7. Plan a mini-celebration, both at work and at home, on the day of or a few days before your actual sabbatical begins. This will give everyone a vivid message that you're departing for a while.

8. Put your other affairs in order, in case something out of the ordinary happens to you during your time away. Update your will, pay bills in advance, and ensure that certain minimum sums are in various checking and savings accounts.

9. Install appropriate messages on your voice mail and in email so that uninformed people who try to contact you aren't left thinking that you're ignoring them.

10. Identify what you need in terms of clothing and implements. If you'll be traveling, consolidate as much as you can. Use the smallest containers and lightest objects.

If you have a specific mission for your sabbatical, such as doing research or volunteering in some capacity, identify in advance as many of the supplies and other tools you'll need to facilitate your efforts. Make checklists as needed.

11. Schedule a complete health checkup so that you leave with a clean bill of health, or at least the cleanest bill of health that you can. Visit your eye doctor, your dentist, and any other doctor with whom it makes sense to have an appointment.

12. If you'll be traveling by car, take your car in for a complete tune-up.

Reflect and Win
Set up a system so that you can stay as informed as you need to be without diminishing the impact of what you want to accomplish during your sabbatical.

The Sabbatical Begins

On that first day, when you don't head into work and your routine is different, you'll probably feel good. Over the next couple days, if you're at home, you might feel rested. You could clean out the freezer, take care of the minor inconveniences that you let slide during the interim, and feel in command of your home.

If it's not a stay-at-home sabbatical—that is, if you're on the road, almost from the opening day, you'll experience what the stay-at-home types experience by about the sixth or seventh day: "My goodness, this *is* different."

Here are do's and don'ts to help you along during these first few impressionable days:

➤ Do allow yourself some extra sleep. Everyone needs some, so there's no use pretending that you don't. However, after a couple days, your need for extra sleep predictably diminishes.

➤ Do allow yourself to try new foods.

➤ Do take a multi-vitamin every day.

➤ Do be open and responsive to new viewpoints, ways of thinking, and ways of accomplishing things.

➤ Do allow yourself to explore, wander, or simply do nothing.

➤ Do feel free to keep a pen and pad or a pocket dictator nearby to capture whatever thoughts strike you.

➤ Do allow yourself the opportunity to simply be.

➤ Don't fall into the trap of seeking to make every day and every moment "productive."

➤ Don't let your exercise routine slide.

➤ Don't be concerned if you feel out of sorts, out of sync, or simply out of it.

➤ Don't feel guilty about the work and people that you've left behind.

➤ Don't second-guess yourself about whether or not to take the sabbatical. The benefits might not appear for a while or even until your return.

How about you? Are you inspired to take control of your time in a way that a small but growing number of others are beginning to discover? Happy time off!

The Time Master Says
The larger your organization the greater the probability that some sabbatical policy is already in place. The terms might differ greatly from one organization to another, from as much as six months off with full pay in some organizations, to an indefinite time off without pay in other organizations, so you won't know until you investigate.

CHAPTER 26

Living in Real Time

In This Chapter:

➤ To live in real time
➤ Staying off the perpetually over-
  whelmed list
➤ What the gurus say
➤ Older and wiser and more in control of
  your time

This chapter poses and answers vital questions: How would your life be if you could tackle problems and challenges as they arise? What would it feel like to engage in conceptual thinking whenever you wanted or needed to? How would you feel if you had a sense of control and ease about each day? The short answer: You would be living in real time.

12 Components of Living in Real Time

Handling messages as they arrive and finishing the task at hand are small but worthwhile achievements, *and* these acts of living in real time are within your reach.

Examine the following 12 components of living in real time, with the realization that each of these is within your grasp.

1. Leave home in the morning with grace and ease. As you know from Chapter 13, "Becoming a Filing Wizard," you can manage the details beforehand. Take care of as many things as possible the night before so that in the morning you have only to shuffle bodies out the door.

2. Focus on the important issues facing your organization, your department or division, and your job or career. As you learned in Chapter 7, "What Matters Most to You?," when you take care of the important things, the others fall into place.

3. Handle and deal with the day's mail upon arrival, keep piles from forming on your desk, and handle phone calls within half a day.

4. Enjoy a leisurely lunch. You understand the importance of completing tasks so that when you depart for lunch, you're actually at lunch. You enjoy your lunch, digest your food better, perform better back on the job, and have a vastly improved gastro-intestinal outlook.

5. End work at a reasonable time, and feel good about what you accomplish each day. This is straight from Chapter 1, "The Overtime Epidemic: How to Nip It In the Bud"; leaving the workday on time and feeling complete is the vital step for permanently winning back your time.

6. Maintain sufficient and up-to-date health, life, disability, and automobile insurance coverage. If you want to live in real time, this is part of the overall picture.

7. File your annual (and any quarterly) income taxes on time. Recognize that taxes are a necessary obligation and will always be levied. Set up a tax log at the start of each year with room for each legitimate deduction, where you can file receipts and documentation. Buy and use tax return software.

8. Take time to be with friends and relatives. People, not things, count most in this life.

9. Stay in shape and at your desired weight. Health and fitness experts say that working out for as little as 30 minutes a day four times a week can keep you comfortably fit. If you're too busy to stay in shape, you're too busy!

10. Make time for hobbies. Revisit that stamp collection, garden, hiking club, or whatever you let slide. Living in real time means enjoying your most rewarding hobbies and pastimes, regularly.

11. Participate monthly in a worthy cause. When you pick the one or two that matter most to you and take action, you feel good about yourself and about how you're spending your time.

12. Drop back at any time, take a long deep breath, collect your thoughts, and renew your spirit—the focus of the remaining chapters.

Once you realize what it means to live in real time—and how far you've strayed from the mark—several steps emerge for catching up with today (or at least this week). Many are deceptively simple, but don't let that obscure the powerful results they offer.

The Irony of Not Taking Breaks

As I travel around the country speaking to organizations, I am struck by the number of people in my audiences who seem perpetually overwhelmed. The irony is that these people could take breaks throughout their days and weeks, but they don't. The biggest obstacle to winning back your time is the unwillingness to allow yourself a break.

I spoke to one group of executives and their spouses, and learned from many spouses that their executive husbands or wives simply do not allow themselves to take a break.

The Miracle Minute

Paradoxically, executives will be more effective if they pause for an extra minute a couple of times each day. This can be done every morning and afternoon—when returning from the water cooler or restroom, before leaving for lunch, or when returning from lunch. And that's the short list.

To steadfastly proceed full-speed through the day without allowing yourself ten minutes to clear your mind all but guarantees you'll be less effective than those who do. Sadly even people who already perceive this need do not allow themselves to meet it.

The Time Master Says

Seven hours and 50 minutes of work plus ten one-minute intervals of rest or reflection in a work day makes you more productive than does eight solid hours of work.

Clarity in Idle Moments

Entrepreneurs, running their own businesses and managing themselves, might be more inclined to take strategic pauses throughout the day—after all, they're in charge of their own schedules. Too often, it isn't necessarily so; the temptation to overwork can be ferocious. Conversely, if you work for others, perhaps a large organization, you might believe that pausing for the total of ten strategic minutes throughout a work day could jeopardize your standing. This misconception is unfounded.

Chuckling at Life

How many times do you let out a good laugh during the day, especially during the work day? Five-year-olds reportedly laugh 113 times a day, on average. 44-year-olds laugh only 11 times per day. Something happens between the ages of five and 44 to reduce the chuckle factor.

Coming to Terms

A gaffe is a mistake.

Once you reach retirement, fortunately, you tend to laugh again. The trick is to live and work at a comfortable pace and have a lot of laughs along the way—at every age. When you proceed through the work day without humor, the days seem longer and difficult. Part of taking control of your life is stepping back and looking at the big picture, being able to see the lighter side of things. Some of your worst gaffes eventually evolve into the things you pleasantly recall—or your best ideas! Pros who survive laugh.

Reclaiming Your Time, Now and Later

The "Winning Back Your Time" Worksheet below includes nine activities: four at work, three after work, and two during vacation time. Each of these activities has a "Lately," a "Short-Term Goal," and a "Long-Term Goal" category. In the Lately column, enter how many times in the past month you have actually done each activity.

In each Goal column, enter how many times you would like to, say, take a slow and leisurely lunch. In the Short-Term Goal category, for example, you could indicate two times per week.

Be realistic when recording what you have been doing. Be reflective in the short-term goal column, marking down what you can realistically achieve. Be visionary in the long-term goal column, marking down what you would ideally like to achieve.

Winning Back Your Time at Work: Today and Tomorrow

Time	Lately	Short Term Goal	Long Term Goal
Extra minutes, taken, daily			
Leisurely lunches taken, weekly			
Hours not rushed, per week			
Full weekends taken, monthly			
Alternate way home taken, monthly			
Fun on way home, monthly			
Telecommuting from home, monthly			
Three-day vacations taken, annually			
Week long vacations taken, annually			

Systemize the procedure: in the weeks and months ahead, review your chart weekly for reinforcement. Then, take breaks such as these throughout the day, week, and year.

You can pause more often when your day is not jam-packed. The Pareto Principle (the "80/20" rule) holds that 80 percent of your activities contribute to only 20 percent of your results. The remaining 20 percent of your activities contribute to the other 80 percent of your results. Take a hardware store for example: About 20 percent of its stock accounts for 80 percent of the revenues; the remaining 80 percent of the stock accounts for only 20 percent of the revenues.

The key to successful retailing is identifying the 20 percent producing the bulk of the revenues. A smart store manager knows to place that 20 percent where it's most accessible, and put the rest where it won't be in the way. As you learn in Chapter 7, you need to identify which activities at work (and in your personal life) support you and bring you the best results. Have the strength to abandon activities that don't benefit you—get rid of that unproductive 80 percent.

What the Gurus Say

Having made it this far in the book, want to know what some of renowned time management authors have advised?

How to Get Control of Your Time and Your Life

This book by Alan Lakein is considered the classic in the field of time management. The information presented in this 1970 book is useful to this day. Lakein offers masterful tips for overcoming procrastination.

Lakein wrote his book, however, when the world population was only half of what it is today. Understandably, he didn't address the changing structure of the family, including the problems of the two-career family and rearing children. Also, he offers little coverage of the impact of technology on the use of time.

Acknowledging that today's readers require new approaches to managing more, Lakein wrote another book called *Give Me a Moment and I'll Change Your Life: Tools for Moment Management*. This book was designed to update the results-oriented approach of his earlier book and explains how to pay attention to moments as they come along and treat time as a limited resource

First Things First: To Live, to Love, to Learn, to Leave a Legacy

First Things First, by Stephen R. Covey, Roger Merrill, and Rebecca Merrill, shows readers how to analyze their use of time and create a balance between their personal and professional responsibilities. The book encourages readers to "put first things first" and act upon them. The authors teach an effective organizing process that helps the reader categorize tasks so that he or she can focus on what is important, not merely what is urgent. The book presents profound insights, such as, "Doing more things faster is no substitute for doing the right things," and the real human needs are "to live, to love, to learn, to leave a legacy."

The quintessential advice is to first categorize your life in four quadrants labeled urgent, not urgent, important, and unimportant. A task might have a deadline but not much importance; or, a task might be important but require preparation and planning. The authors say to stop doing what's unimportant and lacks urgency. Rather, expend your energy where the important and the urgent intersect. Assuming that urgency announces itself, the real issue is "knowing what's important." The authors draw from a variety of sources to guide you toward determining the relative importance of tasks.

The Time Trap

This book by R. Alec MacKenzie was first published many decades ago. It offers time tactics, interviews, and traditional time management tools. Based on the theory that self-management is the key to handling time crunches, it focuses on the author's 20 biggest time wasters, such as telephone interruptions, the inability to say "no," and personal disorganization.

The book offers instructions on how to combat such unnecessary distractions. It also includes information on time problems caused by technology, downsizing, and self-employment. The book's underlying premise is that readers can be taught "how to squeeze the optimal efficiency—and satisfaction—out of their workday."

Time Tactics of Very Successful People

Author Eugene Griessman presents often-cited time management tips, but then reaches beyond that and adds personal insights from well-known and successful people, including business leaders, Nobel laureates, and peak performers.

The time management tactics from those who have achieved successful, balanced lives are presented in short "bites." These tips are designed to inspire today's time-starved readers—whether they're overworked managers, working moms, entrepreneurs on the go, or anyone in need of more time.

Take a Cue from Other Cultures

Some customs in societies throughout the world are well-worth emulating when it comes to finding the time to relax.

➤   In France, it is the legendary two-hour lunch.
➤   In Latin countries, it is the mid-day siesta.
➤   In England, it is tea and crumpets at 4 p.m.
➤   In Japan, it is wearing only slippers once you come home.
➤   In the Aleutian Islands, it is carving ice sculptures.
➤   In Italy, it is having a candlelight dinner and being serenaded by musicians.
➤   In the U.S., it is meeting your team for the softball game.
➤   In Australia, it is putting another shrimp on the "Barbie."

And what about you? Can you withdraw from the madding crowd, have a life during your life, go whole weekends without doing anything, and take true vacations? Can you spend evenings sitting on the porch, as the late John Lennon said, "watching the wheels go round and round?" These are not lost arts.

Here are suggestions for periodically abandoning the rat race, starting with small steps:

➤   Give yourself permission to go a whole weekend without reading anything.
➤   Put your phone on silent and don't retrieve any messages until the next day.
➤   Collect all the magazines piling up around your house, and give them away to a retirement community, library, or school.
➤   Schedule that spa treatment you've been meaning to have.
➤   Exchange photos with a friend you haven't seen in years.

➤ Locate schedules of your favorite professional or amateur teams, and mark on your calendar the appropriate dates to sit back and enjoy the games.

➤ Stroll around a botanical garden to enjoy the variety of flowers; let your sense of smell, rather than your eyes and ears, dominate.

➤ Attend the graduation ceremonies of your local high school. Recapture the spirit of what it was like to complete an important passage in life.

➤ Pick up a bouquet of fresh flowers at the grocery store or flower shop and display them somewhere in your home.

➤ Walk around your yard barefoot. Feel the grass between your toes. Stick your feet in dirt or in a puddle.

➤ Visit a historical monument and let yourself become immersed in the challenges that people of that era faced.

➤ Attend a free lecture some evening on a topic you haven't yet unexplored.

➤ Finally, sleep late.

Pause!

Remember, when you force-fit leisure between barrages of constant frenzy, the quality of your leisure is going to suffer. For that matter, so are you.

Now is a Good Time

Marlee Matlin won the Academy Award for Best Actress at age 21; Jessica Tandy won it at age 80. The U.S. Constitution was written by men who were, on average, 40 years of age—when the life expectancy was barely 40. Sure, some were old-timers like Ben Franklin, but most of the founding fathers were young by today's standards. Regardless of your age or how much time you have left in this life, anytime is a good one to practice measures for winning back your time. Revel in your current age—it holds so much potential.

James Michener didn't write his first novel until age 42. He produced one best-seller after another until his death at age 90.

Reflect and Win

The key to accepting your age and your life is to realize that people shift into high gear at different times. It's hard to predict who's going to take off when.

The End of Your Life: Disappointed or Glad?

Alice Cornyn-Selby, a prolific author and speaker from Portland, Oregon, uses two powerful key phrases with her audiences:

1. "I have now come to the end of my life and I'm disappointed that I didn't _____."

How did you finish that sentence? Whatever came up first is probably something you want to do right away. No use putting it off any longer, because it bubbled up to the surface immediately.

2. "I have now come to the end of my life and I'm glad that I _____."
   What did you come up with this time? Was it the same issue that you addressed in the first statement? Was it something you've already accomplished? When you begin to look at the opportunities that await and those you can create, all the rushing about that came before and the times you felt you were missing your life can begin to melt away as you head in the direction that will give you deep satisfaction.

Whether you're 20 or 80, or in between, it's time to start looking at your life as if the best years are yet to come, for indeed they can be coming. Sure, you'll become a little slower with each advancing year, but you have the ability to draw upon the wisdom you've learned in each decade. Perhaps you'll be even more prudent with your time.

CHAPTER 27

Keeping It All in Perspective

In This Chapter:

➤ Full bore no more
➤ True productivity is measured by results
➤ Lingering at crucial moments
➤ Pacing yourself

In this last chapter, you'll learn why keeping the tasks in your work and the events in your life in perspective yields great benefits.

When I speak to groups or consult with individuals, I am amazed at some of the time pressure stories they tell me. The number of items competing for their time and attention and the schedules they're trying to balance and juggle would leave me in a tizzy.

When I ask them how things got to be so hectic, many respond in a way that mystifies me. Their response is similar to the situation where you walk into a room and see a child and a broken toy. You ask the child what happened to the toy. He simply shrugs and says, "It broke."

Adults who are continually racing the clock are acting in ways analogous to the child who claims, "It broke." Such adults are taking little responsibility for their hectic lives. They claim that they're victims of circumstance.

Stop Creating Pressure for Yourself

Unquestionably, the world is becoming more demanding. As much as anyone, I am aware the information and communication bombardment the typical individual experiences on any given day.

Nevertheless, in proceeding through work and life, presumably one begins to understand the importance of *being more selective, becoming and staying organized, saying no, maintaining balance,* and *living in the moment.*

Too many people proceed as if they've never heard of these notions or, if they have, they pay them very short shrift. Such people proceed at full bore; they don't seem to have established, let alone pursued priorities; hardly ever say no; and shortchange themselves of essential nutrition, relaxation, and sleep. They seem to convey the message, "The toy is breaking more each day, and I can't understand why. Soon it'll be shattered to pieces."

Living in the moment remains one of the least understood, infrequently addressed, seldom used, human capabilities. Too few individuals have any experience or knowledge of living in the moment; it is lost among a flurry of activity—"busy-ness."

Living in the moment means being aware of your power in the present. While it is not a complete recipe for winning back your time, it helps greatly. It is being able observe the finely woven canvas of your career while you are in progress. It is giving yourself permission to be who you are. It is resting when you're tired. It is not constantly striving.

Freed from the preoccupation that limits your experience of the present, you could feel more present than you have in years, with better focus and more resolve.

Coming to Terms

Living in the moment means proceeding through your day with vibrant expression and keen perception, with an intense awareness of your surroundings. It's getting to work each day with the thought, "I'm alive, and this day is only starting."

Once you realize what it means to dwell in real time and how far you could have strayed from the mark, there are several things you can do to begin to catch up with today (or at least this week). Many are deceptively simple, but don't let that obscure the powerful results they offer. Foremost is allowing yourself to take time-outs at work as you deem them to be necessary.

Pause to Stay Competitive

From individuals to large organizations, speeding through the day or year has its drawbacks, and pausing to reflect, to learn, and to grow has its benefits.

One corporation discovered that a little instruction here and there didn't educate their employees the way they had hoped. It certainly didn't stick with their employees. So the company started its own university with its own staff of 300 instructors and an initial annual budget of $60 million, and developed in-house programs and long-term alliances with local colleges.

Why such elaborate procedures? They were implemented to help the organization stay competitive. Similarly, for you to stay competitive, pause periodically throughout the day, every day.

Leaders Know When to Pause

Some of the most productive and energetic people in history learned how to pace themselves effectively by taking a few "time outs" each day. Thomas Edison would rest for a few minutes each day when he felt his energy level dropping.

Buckminster Fuller often worked in cycles of three or four hours, slept for 30 minutes, and then repeated the process. He found that in the course of a 24-hour period, he would get far more done than if he had followed traditional waking and sleeping patterns. While this approach isn't for everyone, it worked for Bucky. By giving himself rest at shorter intervals, Fuller was able to extend his productive hours.

Pause!
Top achievers employ periodic pauses so that they can return to their activities with more energy and focus than they had, right before the chose to pause!

Take Advantage of Alertness Mapping

For most people, the time when they are least alert is between 2:00 a.m. and 5:00 a.m. Highest alertness is between 9:00 a.m. and noon, and between 4:00 p.m. to 8:00 p.m. Your alertness will vary depending on your own physiology and inclinations, as well as on the hours of consecutive duty, hours of duty in the preceding week, irregular hours, monotony on the job, timing and duration of naps, sound, aroma, temperature, environmental lighting, sleep deprivation over the past week, and much more.

Seek time intervals within your own work week, and even weekend, when you are fully alert and can be more productive with your time.

Finding Clarity in Idle Moments

Entrepreneurs, running their own businesses and managing themselves, allegedly would be more inclined to take strategic pauses throughout the day; after all, they're in charge of their own schedule. Too often, it isn't necessarily so. The temptation to overwork can be ferocious.

Conversely, if you work for others, perhaps a large organization, you could erroneously believe that pausing for the total of ten strategic minutes throughout a work day could somehow jeopardize your standing. This misconception is unfounded.

Reflect and Win

The CEOs in many top organizations routinely take naps at midday to recharge their batteries. They have executive assistants who shield them from the outside world, take their calls, and arrange their schedules while they snooze.

If you are not the CEO of a large organization, the thought of being able to take a nap in the middle of the workday could seem like Nirvana to you. Yet, the ten strategic minutes I have recommended provide a similar benefit in your quest to stay in control. If you can't take a flat-out nap, ten well-placed minutes could be your best alternative.

Take Your Foot off the Throttle

You can't charge through the day full throttle and expect to be at your peak level all the while. Be realistic. You need to regularly take breaks, at least half a minute or so every 20 minutes, and a good three- or four-minute break at a minimum every hour, to ensure that you stay sharp, stimulate your circulation, and take care of necessities.

In general, any time you feel yourself getting bogged down with all the tasks you need to complete in the day, take a walk or switch to another task for which you have sufficient energy. Do anything else which will help to minimize tension, keep you alert, and help you to stay more productive throughout the remainder of the day. Think of it this way: execute, reflect, reevaluate, and proceed. As lunch time approaches, reevaluate what you've done, and how you plan to proceed during the afternoon.

The Time Master Says

If you find yourself easily distracted at work, experiment with the times in which you tackle certain tasks. Maybe it makes sense for you to come in an hour earlier than everyone else, or to stay an hour later. Maybe it makes sense for you to eat lunch at a different time so that you can work during the usual lunch hour.

Break Up Your Week

If you can work off-site one day a week, or depending on your organization, only once every two weeks, you'll be in a good position to accomplish certain types of tasks more adroitly than in the traditional office.

Also, if you're able to telecommute, using your phone and e-mail to stay in touch with your office, you've saved commuting time and wear and tear on your car, prolonged the length of your wardrobe, and afforded yourself the opportunity to get an extra half-hour of sleep the night before. What's more, you've established an environment where you can work efficiently.

Seek New Sources of Input

Have you ever eaten lunch with a colleague and begun discussing ways to approach your work more effectively? After a few minutes, you're both deep into the conversation, coming up with all sorts of great ideas on how to sail through the day. However, when the waiter comes to take your order or bring your check, what happens? The conversation dies down.

When you each head back to work, those ideas are often forgotten or put on a back burner. If you consciously schedule a meeting for the sole purpose of letting the creative sparks fly, you'll grab control of your time and have some of the most productive sessions you've ever had.

I met with a mentor once a month in his dining room. At a cleared table, we sat across from each other with an audio recorder, discussing problems and issues that we faced and ways we could overcome them. Each of us kept a copy of the recording and took notes from it. We captured those ideas instead of letting them die.

Seek other ways to shake up your routine for the insights and breakthroughs that could result. Every day and each moment holds great potential in winning back your time.

Reflect and Win

When you come in contact with other people, you're exposed to whole new worlds, their worlds. When you interact with another person, you get the benefit of his/her information, in addition to your own.

The Perspective of a View from Above

Think about flying on an airplane. You have a window seat, and it's a clear day. As you gaze down to the ground below, what do you see? Cars the size of ants. Miniature baseball diamonds. Hotels that look like Monopoly pieces. Life passing by.

The same effect can take place at the top of a mountain or a skyscraper. As often as possible, when things seem to be racing by too fast, get to higher ground for a clear perspective of what needs to be accomplished.

If you're among the lucky, perhaps you regularly allocate time for reflection or meditation. If you don't, no matter. There are other ways to slow it all down. After the workday, listen to relaxing music with headphones and with your eyes closed. A half hour of your favorite music with no disturbances (and your eyes closed) can seem almost endless. When you re-emerge, the rest of the day takes on a different tone and you are able to get more done than you would have at your previous level of alertness.

Keep Fighting for Perspective

By altering our personal perspectives—our perceptions, our response to stimuli, even the pace at which we proceed throughout the day—we have the opportunity to engage in our careers in a manner that is more manageable, less complex, and more enjoyable. The key is to develop a mindset that both acknowledges the multitude of items competing for one's time and attention and concurrently acknowledge that one has the capabilities and the intelligence to rise above the fray.

You possess the distinct capability to adopt seemingly minor work-style changes that result in both productivity and peace of mind. Here are some thoughts worth pondering:

➤ Much of what seems urgent and compelling is not.
➤ Sometimes the best strategy for facing challenging tasks is to slow down.
➤ You have the ability to pause momentarily throughout the day to mentally, emotionally, and spiritually renew yourself.
➤ Your actions can have a calming effect on those around you.
➤ Satisfaction with your work and your life can come in a nearly continual stream.

Winning back your time is more a mind set than a set of procedures. You have the power to alter your thinking and your surroundings so as to accomplish what you want and to maintain a sense of work-life balance.

BIBLIOGRAPHY

Cameron, Julia, *The Artist's Way* (Tarcher, 1992).

Cathcart, Jim, *The Acorn Principle* (St. Martin's, 1999).

Covey, Stephen, *The Seven Habits of Highly Effective Families* (Franklin/Covey, 1997).

Csikszentmihalyi, Mihaly, *Flow: The Psychology of Optimal Experience* (Harper, 1990).

Davidson, Jeff, *Breathing Space: Living & Working at a Comfortable Pace in a Sped-up Society* (CreateSpace, 2007).

Davidson, Jeff, *Dial it Down, Live it Up* (Sourcebooks, 2014).

Davidson, Jeff, *Simpler Living* (Skyhorse Publishing, 201).

Davidson, Jeff, *The 60 Second Innovator* (Adams Media, 2009).

Davidson, Jeff, *The 60 Second Organizer* (Adams Media, 2008).

Davidson, Jeff, *The Smart Guide to Getting Things Done* (Smart Guide Publications, 2015)..

Davidson, Jeff, *The Smart Guide to Winning Back Your Time* (Smart Guide Publications, 2015).

Diamond, Dr. John, *Your Body Doesn't Lie: How to Increase Your Life Energy Through Behavioral Kinesiology* (Warner, 1994).

Dement, William, *The Promise of Sleep* (Delacort, 1999).

Dominguez, Joe, and Vicki Robin, *Your Money or Your Life* (Viking, 1992).

Drucker, Peter, *The Effective Executive* (Harper & Row, 1967).

Dychtwald, Ken, Ph.D., *Age Wave* (Tarcher, 1989).

Farrell, Dr. Warren, *Why Men are the Way They Are* (McGraw-Hill, 1986).

Friedan, Betty, *The Fountain of Age* (Simon & Schuster, 1993).

Fritz, Robert, *The Path of Least Resistance* (Fawcett Columbine, 1989).

Griessman, Eugene, *Time Tactics of Very Successful People* (McGraw-Hill, 1994).

Gross, Irma and Mary Lewis, *Home Management* (out of print, 1938).

Jeffers, Susan, *Feel the Fear and Do It Anyway* (Harcourt, Brace & Jovanovich, 1987).

Johnson, Magic, *My Life* (Random House, 1992).

Kanter, Rosabeth Moss, *The Change Masters* (Simon & Schuster, 1983).

Kawasaki, Guy, *How to Drive the Competition Crazy* (Hyperion, 1995).

Kostner, Dr. Jaclyn, *Virtual Leadership* (Warner, 1996).

Kutner, Lawrence, *Your School-Age Child* (Morrow, 1996).

Lakein, Alan, *How to Get Control of Your Time and Your Life* (New American Library, 1973).

Lasn, Kalle, *Culture Jamming* (Morrow, 1999).

MacKenzie, R. Alec, *The Time Trap* (AMACOM, 1997).

Moore-Ede, Martin, M.D., Ph.D., *The 24-Hour Society* (Addison-Wesley, 1993).

Postman, Neil, Ph.D., *Amusing Ourselves to Death* (Viking, 1985).

Postman, Neil, Ph.D., *Technopoly* (Knopf, 1992).

Proat, Frieda, *Creative Procrastination* (Harper & Row, 1980).

Rajineesh, Osho, *Don't Just Do Something, Sit There* (Maineesha, 1980).

Rifkin, Jeremy, *Time Wars* (Henry Holt, 1987).

Rose, Kenneth, *The Organic Clock* (Wiley, 1988).

Shenkman, Richard, *Legends, Lies, and Cherished Myths of American History* (Morrow, 1989).

Taylor, Frederic, *The Principles of Scientific Management* (Harper & Row, 1911).

Thomas, Stanley, *The Millionaire Next Door* (Dearborn, 1999).

Toffler, Alvin, *Future Shock* (Random House, 1970).

Twitchell, James, *Carnival Culture* (Columbia University Press, 1992).

Waitely, Denis, *Timing is Everything* (Pocket Books, 1993).

GLOSSARY

Contrarian—Somebody who opts to engage in activities at times and places in which no one else is engaging them.

Cookie—An electronic marker that a Web site places on your hard drive so that if/when you revisit the Web site, your PC is electronically recognized; you might be directed towards Web site features that presumably lie within your area of interest.

Dynamic bargain—An agreement you make with yourself to assess what you've accomplished (and what more you want to accomplish) from time to time throughout the day, adjusting to new conditions as they emerge.

Faustian bargains—Shady deals, so named after the lead character in *Doctor Faustus* who sold his eternal soul to the devil for a better time on earth.

Ergonomics—The science that examines how devices most smoothly blend with the human body and human activity.

Formulating—In the context of answering email, ensuring to the best of one's ability that the message is clear and accurate and conveys precisely what the sender wishes to communicate.

Hydration—When your body's tissues are sufficiently filled with water. To be dehydrated is to be parched.

Insidious—Something that is treacherous.

Leisure—Enjoying rewarding activities free from work and preoccupation with work.

Living in the moment—Proceeding through your day with vibrant expression and keen perception, with an intense awareness of your surrounding.

Microsleep—A 5-to-10-second episode when your brain is effectively asleep while you are otherwise up and about. Microsleep can occur while you are working at your PC or driving a car.

Midnight—Originally halfway through the night because people went to sleep when it got dark around 7 p.m. or 8 p.m. and got up when it became light around 5 a.m.

Netiquette—The combination of the words net and etiquette form the new word, which means online etiquette.

Opt-out capability—The ability to easily select to be removed from a spammer's list.

Overchoice—The stress that comes from too many options, especially the "so-what?" variety.

Piddling—Something that it is paltry, trivial, or inconsequential.

Rapid eye movements (REM)—When sleeping, your eyes actually shift all over although your eyelids are closed; these movements and various levels of brain activity are essential to sound sleep.

Restoration—A conversion or return of something that was missing. The process of being made whole again.

Schlepping—A Yiddish word that means over-extending yourself, often in the context of accomplishing small tasks.

Seed work—Tasks you can easily assign to someone else because the downside risk if he or she botches the task is negligible.

Self-storage unit—A for-rent, garage-like space you can fill with any items you don't need too often.

Sound screen—An electronic device that creates a sound "barrier," which masks or mutes the effects of sound from beyond the barrier.

Spate—A large number or amount.

Stock message—A prepared reply that you store in your templates, draft, or signature folder to re-use as the situation applies.

Telecommuting—Working outside the office (away from your employer's base of operations) and staying in touch with coworkers via electronics, such as a computer, fax, and phone.

Tickler files—A file system designed to give you a place to chronologically park items related to forthcoming issues and remind you when you need to deal with such issues.

Time cost—Also known as potential efficiency cost, this is the time you lose by switching from one task to another.

Triage—The practice of quickly examining a variety of items and allocating them based on what needs to be handled immediately, what can be handled later, and what can be ignored altogether.

White noise—A non-invasive, non-disruptive sound (much like that of rushing water, a fan, or a distant motor).

Made in the USA
Middletown, DE
01 July 2015